What people are saying about …

TURNAROUND
AT HOME

"Jack and Lisa Hibbs have a heart to see families live up to what God
has intended. With bold hope and fresh insight, they show us how
to 'put on the brakes' in an unhealthy home environment and how
to move into the future with spiritual and emotional fitness. This
book is a balance of spiritual, God-given principles and practical,
God-inspired examples. By reading it I believe your own heart will
grow bigger toward your God and your family."

Skip Heitzig, senior pastor of Calvary
Albuquerque in Albuquerque, NM

"It has been well said that 'as the family goes, so goes the nation,
and so goes the whole world in which we live.' As we look across
the American family landscape we can all agree that families are
struggling to stay afloat. But cheer up—help is on the way! In their
book *Turnaround at Home*, Jack and Lisa let us in on their own
personal experiences, setbacks, victories, and what you can do to
ensure that you give your children a greater family legacy than what
you've received."

Greg Laurie, senior pastor of Harvest
Christian Fellowship in Riverside, CA

"A civilization either rises or falls based upon one interesting fact. You may find it surprising that it is not predicated upon its economic wealth or prosperity. Nor is it based upon its military prowess or ability to create laws and/or institutions of higher education. All of those things, needless to say, are important, but without the foundation of a strong, loving family, none of those things work to establish a solid nation. In a day and age where families are devalued and of little importance, this book seeks to turn us around and point us back to the importance not only of teaching biblical family values but also of living them out within the family unit."

Tony Perkins, president of Family
Research Council in Washington DC

TURN
AROUND
AT HOME

FOREWORD BY CHUCK SMITH

TURN AROUND AT HOME

GIVING A STRONGER SPIRITUAL LEGACY
THAN YOU RECEIVED

JACK & LISA HIBBS
WITH KURT BRUNER

DAVID C COOK

transforming lives together

TURNAROUND AT HOME
Published by David C Cook
4050 Lee Vance Drive
Colorado Springs, CO 80918 U.S.A.

Integrity Music Limited, a Division of David C Cook
Brighton, East Sussex BN1 2RE, England

The graphic circle C logo is a registered trademark of David C Cook.

The website addresses recommended throughout this book are offered as a
resource to you. These websites are not intended in any way to be or imply an
endorsement on the part of David C Cook, nor do we vouch for their content.

Library of Congress Control Number 2013946264
ISBN 978-0-7814-1031-1
eISBN 978-1-4347-0719-2

© 2013 Jack Hibbs, Lisa Hibbs, and Kurt Bruner
The author is represented by MacGregor Literary, Inc. of Hillsboro, OR.

The Team: John Blase, Nick Lee, Caitlyn Carlson, Karen Athen
Cover Design: Amy Konyndyk
Cover Photo: Veer Images

Printed in the United States of America
First Edition 2013

5 6 7 8 9 10 11 12 13 14

060721

CONTENTS

Authors' Note

We want to express appreciation to individuals who helped make this book possible, including those who let us share their turnaround stories. Some of the names and circumstances have been changed to give us the freedom to relay potentially embarrassing details and/or unpack the real-world impact of these principles.

This book has been a collaborative effort with Dr. J. Otis Ledbetter and Kurt Bruner. Dr. Ledbetter provided invaluable insight forged over decades of ministering to families. A respected author and cofounder of Heritage Builders, he leads an international ministry that helps parents pass a strong spiritual legacy on to the next generation. Dr. Ledbetter's teachings and writings serve as a foundation for much of what you will find in this book.

Our coauthor, Kurt Bruner, is a bestselling author who spent twenty years working with one of our heroes, Dr. James Dobson. As vice president of Focus on the Family, Kurt led the teams that created practical tools for families, including the popular *Adventures in Odyssey* series. Over the past several years he has led a growing movement of churches, including our own, in working to create a culture of intentional families.

This book was written *about* people *for* people. It recognizes that how we relate to one another today grows out of our individual upbringings. People can be hard to live with. *We can be hard to live with!* It is our desire that the following pages will help you move beyond your present reality toward God's best for you and your family. The Bible has much to say about how we are to relate to one another, and we would do well to pay attention.

How we were raised manifests itself in how we act, react, and demonstrate love in our present relationships. Even as Christians, as new creations in Christ, we can struggle with painful past childhood issues. But we don't need to let our pasts negatively affect our children's futures—nor should we.

Those of us with grown children may wish we could have a do-over. Of course that is not possible. So we encourage you to change the future rather than drown in regrets over the past. Instead of looking back, why not look ahead? God gives each one of us the incredible gift of His mercies, which are new every morning.

We know this firsthand. By God's grace, our children are now raising their own children in a more loving and thoughtful way than we raised them. For that we are grateful.

Over the course of our thirty-four years of marriage, our diverse backgrounds brought about a lively and vigorous energy to the truth that God makes two people into one flesh. After over two decades of pastoral ministry, we have learned a great deal about the enormous and loving plan God has for each family as they choose to follow His ways.

We trust that this book will help you begin to understand that you can't change the heritage you were given, but you can change the heritage you will give to the next generation. As you allow yourself to glean what you can from the past while looking forward with hope to the future, we pray that the words of the apostle Paul will be true in each of your lives.

Not that I have already attained, or am already perfected; but I press on, that I may lay hold of that for which Christ Jesus has also laid hold of me. Brethren, I do not count myself to have apprehended; but one thing I do, forgetting those things which are behind and reaching forward to those things which are ahead, I press toward the goal for the prize of the upward call of God in Christ Jesus. (Phil. 3:12–14)

Jack and Lisa Hibbs
May 2013

FOREWORD

Far too many Christian leaders have sacrificed their families in the name of building a "successful" ministry. But God established the home before He established the church. He called parents to bring up children in the faith before He called pastors to equip the saints.

Since the beginning of time, God has placed a high value upon the institution of the family. He has communicated to us in such a personal way, referring to Himself as our Father and calling us His children.

The Bible tells us that God said, "Let us make man in our image, after our likeness" (Gen. 1:26 ESV). He told Adam, Eve, and their children that they were to have dominion over all of creation. He delighted in the formation of the family, and He proclaimed that it was good. He engineered the family as the nucleus of mankind, and He blessed both male and female with the ability to "be fruitful and multiply" (1:28). Simply put, God created us to flourish within the dynamic of family life. It was His idea from the start.

Unfortunately the family structure that was ordained by God has been the target of attack. Our enemy wants to keep every family from fulfilling God's designed purpose of passing down a godly heritage. When he succeeds in that effort, serious damage is done to the faith of future generations.

The family is a living, breathing organism and has been established as the place in which God's love, His Word, and His grace can be experienced in a tangible manner. It's where we learn submission, authority, compassion, discipline, and instruction. The home is where it all begins.

Henry Drummond once said that "the family circle is the supreme conductor of Christianity." God is the One who created parents to be His instruments for molding and shaping another generation of believers. Yet many Christian parents struggle to become loving examples of Christianity in their homes. They fail to give themselves over to God's purpose and plan, thus repeating the same negative cycles they saw in their own homes while growing up.

God said in Deuteronomy 5 that the sins of the guilty will impact their children (v. 9). But He went on to say that He will show loving-kindness to the descendants of those who love and obey Him (v. 10). Yes, the "sins of the fathers" continue on into future generations because of the impact of what those future generations have observed. But when the power of God's glorious Word is introduced into a life, it breaks that destructive cycle. Jesus Christ and the gospel can transform a life. By God's grace, He re-creates and restores a man or woman and places him or her back on the course He intended. There is nothing more encouraging for me than to see ruined lives dramatically changed and used mightily by God! That kind of turnaround in a life is nothing short of a miracle. And every changed life also means a changed family and changed future generations.

To anyone who is willing to make a change and break the cycle in his or her life, this book offers encouragement and hope. We all need to honestly look at the legacy we were given. We all need to turn around to embrace the good that God intends for us. And we all need to cast aside any destructive influences that were handed down to us from our parents so that those influences don't continue into the next generation. Unhealthy cycles can then be broken through faith in Jesus Christ and by following God's will for the home. I know you will find hope and healing in the pages that follow as you take steps toward experiencing God's unfailing love in your family.

Chuck Smith, Senior Pastor
Calvary Chapel Costa Mesa
Costa Mesa, California

CHAPTER ONE

TURNAROUND

I lay the sins of the parents upon their children; the entire family is affected—even children in the third and fourth generations of those who reject me. But I lavish unfailing love for a thousand generations on those who love me and obey my commands.

Deuteronomy 5:9b–10 (NLT)

When Dave proposed to Stephanie, only four hours had passed since they first met on the beautiful East Coast seaboard. Soon their whirlwind romance brought them across the country, landing them briefly in Las Vegas for their wedding. Stephanie was pregnant with their first child, and Dave had only recently been discharged from the military. Dave's dog tag read *Catholic* while Stephanie's confusing background blended a bit of exuberant Pentecostal with reserved Baptist. Neither, however, knew the first thing about raising a child or what a healthy, God-fearing household actually looked like.

When Dave was in the third grade, his parents divorced. Before that, they spent most of their days yelling and screaming at each other. Dave was so devastated by their breakup that, as a young man, he made a solemn vow: when he had children of his own, he would never put them through the same pain that he had experienced. Unfortunately, his parents provided him a poor example of how to avoid ruining his own future relationships. In fact, the best counsel he could remember receiving from his father was when he told Dave never to get any girls pregnant as he handed over a box of condoms.

Stephanie, on the other hand, grew up in the Bible Belt, where the fear of the Lord was ever present—but a strong, healthy understanding of God's Word was not. Her father had been killed in prison when she was a young girl, which forced her, her mother, and her two siblings to move in with her grandmother and step-grandfather. It was there that her step-grandfather began to sexually abuse her between the ages of five and nine. Her grandmother, completely unaware of the abuse, constantly reinforced to Stephanie that she would go to hell if she ever had sex before getting married. On the other hand, her mother began taking her to clubs by the age of seventeen, encouraging her that it was important to sleep with a guy before she married him to make sure that everything would work out—no doubt a very mixed message for a young, impressionable girl.

After Stephanie married Dave, she made a vow the same way Dave had when his parents divorced: to end the cycle of abuse and pain she'd endured. She was determined to give her children something better than she had been given as a child. The problem? She had absolutely no clue what that would look like. And Dave was no help. He became an alcoholic, partying often with his friends and eventually cheating on Stephanie. Within a few short years, their marriage was in shambles and headed straight for divorce, dooming each of them to break their respective promises. And the ones who would pay the price? Their children. Indeed, the sin of the parents was now at work in their home.

AS THE FAMILY GOES ...

Look around you. Unfortunately, Dave and Stephanie's tragic story isn't an isolated one. God's prized creation—the family—has been corrupted, attacked, ridiculed, and made nearly obsolete. It is crumbling away, and there seems to be no way to stop the assault. Human wisdom tries to intervene, but it seems to only drive us further and further away from God's ultimate design. The church has tried to fix it, but its own members have become just as much victims of the onslaught as everyone else.

Family: ripped apart, redefined, and struggling to rediscover its significance. None of this is part of God's plan. In the beginning, God created Adam and Eve—the first family—and they were the first things in all His great work to be called "very good." That's exactly what God had intended the family to be: very good! Throughout the Bible, we see God using the institution of marriage and family to communicate His great love toward His people.

He told us from the beginning to be fruitful and multiply, to honor our fathers and our mothers, and to serve the Lord in our homes. Yet an ever-increasing number of children are growing up in homes that have veered from that plan. Homes are no longer "very good," and they bear the battle scars to prove it. Divorce, abusive words and deeds, legalism without love, and a pseudolove without boundaries seem to prevail instead.

But thankfully, there is hope. There is a way to set things in order, and it all starts with a turnaround in our own homes.

We've been given the power to change the nation—and the world—through the grace and knowledge of Jesus Christ. But how does that happen? It happens when one individual, through the power of the Holy Spirit, stops the flow and direction in which he or she was heading. It might be a father who decides to row against the downstream pull of the river—or a mother who chooses to change the path and course that were passed down to her.

There is an old saying: "As the family goes, so goes the nation." This is so true! The family has been spiraling out of control for so many years now that it's no wonder our nation is in the condition it's in. But if we will intentionally encourage and train our families, as God intended us to do, we'll see a tremendous change in our land, one household at a time.

Changing the direction of a home is possible. Lisa and I know because we've experienced it. The power of God's Word will lead that change if we are willing to yield completely to Him. We can all thank God that He is a God of second chances. The fact that we can change, that we can have the opportunity to turn things around, is an amazing display of His grace. But we must be willing to move from what is wrong to what is right, to shift from what isn't working to what will work. In a word, we need a change.

SHIFTING DIRECTIONS

The ancient Greeks used the word *metanoeo* when it came to sailing a ship. The word means "to change direction or to think differently." It's a full course correction. A complete turnaround from the direction in which you were heading. It's from this ancient understanding that we get our English word *repent*, which means to change your mind. Jesus said, "Repent and believe," meaning, "Stop unbelieving and believe."

It's unfortunate that the concept and definition of the word *repent* have gotten a bad rap throughout the years, but it is actually a very positive word. To change our minds about how we were raised is our first step in turning around our own homes. We must reverse our course and head toward a new standard—God's standard.

None of us were raised in perfect homes. We all carry baggage of a past we just can't seem to shake or some sort of a legacy we didn't ask for. All of this has the annoying side effect of influencing the everyday decisions we make that impact our future.

So consider this: What kind of home were you raised in? We will examine this more fully in chapters 4 through 7 because it does make a difference. Unless you make a concerted effort to change the way you think and feel about certain things, then how you were raised will have a direct impact on how you in turn raise your own children.

Most of us experienced a mixture of positive and negative aspects in our home life, but unfortunately the line between those two is not always clear.

Typically there are two ways that we handle our pasts.

1. Define It as the "New Normal"

Without a godly example of what parenting should or shouldn't be, our pasts become the standard by which we live. We allow our pasts to define who we are, and this then sets the benchmark for what is considered normal. That would be great if normal was defined as a loving, God-honoring home. It's not so great if your home was filled with dysfunction that you may still not even recognize.

Consider Mark. By the age of thirteen, he was drinking beer with his parents as they played cards. Thirteen! Mark became a full-blown alcoholic by the time he was eighteen. Why? Because his mother and father were alcoholics. Drinking was the norm in his household—and, in fact, his mother and father had "inherited" this behavior from their parents, also alcoholics.

The sins of the parents will be passed down to the third and fourth generations, according to Deuteronomy 5. Abusers tend to beget abusers. Or, as they say, the apple doesn't fall far from the tree. But negative cycles can stop.

2. DESPISE IT COMPLETELY

The second way of handling the past is the flip side of the first. Rather than embrace your past and continue in its shortcomings, you overreact and rebel, rejecting both the bad and the good. If you grew up in a home you despised, you may have a tendency to vow you'll never make the same mistakes your parents made. So if your parents were strict, you may decide to become the most lenient parent, afraid to administer any form of discipline, and thus would end up trading one extreme for another.

IMAGINE

What does a healthy family look like? What defines that which is truly normal and should be embraced and passed on to the benefit of your children versus that which is harmful and should be abandoned and rejected? For that, we must turn to God's Word.

Is it any wonder that Scripture calls God our Father in heaven over and over? Is it any surprise that the relationship of a husband and wife is compared to Christ and His bride, the church? Throughout Scripture, the home is shown to be a husband and wife modeling the loving authority of God for their children. For what purpose, you may ask? So that we would raise up children in the grace and knowledge of Jesus Christ.

John Lennon once sang a song where he asked us to imagine a different kind of world. Unfortunately, his theology was very wrong. He imagined a world without religion and without God, where everyone supposedly lived in harmony. But the kind of harmony he dreamed of can never be realized by rejecting God. It will come only when we each fulfill our part in reflecting God.

Let's imagine instead a world where a model of true Christianity was being followed in the home. What might happen if a father turned himself around and became the dad and husband God intended him to be? What would that look like?

Imagine if a mother turned herself around ... or a grandparent. What if we raised our children to actually live the Christian life according to what the Bible says? How might that impact not only the church, but the secular world as well? We would become messengers of hope to our churches, our culture, and our nation by living out what we believe. This is what revival looks like.

Let me clear something up: revival does not come by first changing the world. That is a misconception. There are many Christians today who believe that revival means changing the hearts of the lost toward God. But that's inaccurate because revival comes, first and foremost, to the house of God—His people. We see it repeatedly throughout the Bible in examples such as Nehemiah, Josiah, and Hezekiah. First, these men personally renewed themselves in the Lord, and then they set out to influence their culture and their nation for what was right. It started with just one individual unabashedly willing to turn back to God, and soon an entire generation of God's people did the same. Only after these leaders began to seek the ways of the Lord was there a profound cultural shift. It happened as well in America's great awakenings. In each case, there was a ripple effect. A radical awakening, a change, repentance, that took place in God's people, bringing about a dramatic shift to the culture at large. The result was a witness to the lost, which brought salvation to many.

Remember Mark? Raised by alcoholics, devoid of any spiritual training, he grew into an adult who didn't know or care what God thought. The same was true for his parents, his siblings, even his grandparents. It wasn't that they didn't believe God existed; it's that they had no idea there was anything better for their lives. They were stuck in the cycle of the sins of the fathers visiting their children. It's all they knew.

But then something happened in Mark's life. After getting his girlfriend, Jill, pregnant, he decided to do the "right thing" and marry her. Jill was a struggling Christian who had desperately wanted to turn things around in her own life but had no idea how. So she asked Mark to go to church with her. To her surprise, he ended up accepting Christ. Within a year, he had completely abandoned his alcoholic past forever! Together they decided to leave their respective godless, emotionally scarred pasts and instead do things differently for their kids. Over the next twenty-plus years, Mark was able to watch his children come to Christ—as well as his sister, his brother, his father, his mother, and even his grandmother! This all happened because of the decision of one person to turn things around.

A PERSONAL REVIVAL

But before we take on the world, we must take on the family. There must be an intentional decision to do things God's way in our own lives. As a result of that, our children will be open to the things of God, and they will be supernaturally blessed!

Wonder whatever happened to Dave and Stephanie? The story of their turnaround is a dramatic one. Stephanie had written her husband off as a loser who would never change. As she was waiting for her divorce to be finalized, a neighbor encouraged her to attend her church, Calvary Chapel. After a few weeks, Stephanie realized that for the first time in her life, she wasn't just "going to church"—she was actually learning what the Word of God said and, more importantly, what it meant.

Almost immediately, Dave started to notice something different about her. This "church thing" interested him, and he soon started attending with her. That's when Dave professed faith in Christ, and within a few short months he had become a new man. At first, Stephanie wasn't too sure about the sincerity of his newfound conversion. But then his life began to truly transform. And so did their marriage. He moved back home in the middle of summer, was baptized a couple of months later, and then completely stopped drinking!

Today, sixteen years later, they are very happily married with three children who love the Lord. Stephanie and Dave actually became the fulfillment of their own personal revivals: they have truly given their children something far better than they had received. But how did they do it?

First, they dedicated and completely surrendered their hearts and lives to the Lord Jesus Christ. They repented of their bitterness, anger, and unforgiveness of past hurts and chose to forgive each other instead. This is an important part of reconciliation with the Lord and with others. There really is no way to turn around completely without an experience with almighty God. He alone gives us the power that we need as He changes us first from the inside out.

Second, they made a commitment to find out what God says in His Word and what they were to be doing with their own lives personally and then in their relationship with each other. They learned that selfishly living their own lives apart from God would never change anything in their home.

They began reading their Bibles as a part of their daily walks with the Lord, praying and serving each other in their home whenever they could. They wanted their children to see that they loved the Lord first and foremost in their individual lives, separate from each other. They attended church faithfully and started serving whenever they saw a need. This enabled them to grow in ways they had yet to understand. Their children have grown up seeing their unwavering commitment to the things of God. And even though the Lord blessed their family financially, they had a strong understanding that it all came from Him and that they needed to give back to others less fortunate than themselves.

Their children were often seen helping alongside them as they gave of their time and resources to help the homeless, the poor, and the down-and-out. Dave and Stephanie raised their children with a good balance of not only knowing the Word but also understanding how to live it out in their everyday lives. And guess what? Their two oldest children are great proponents against drug and alcohol abuse! They truly believe that strong family values and serving God through ministry to others are critical to a strong family that can endure the trials of life. Stephanie and Dave have been and continue to be examples to us and to those who know them as they live out a life of forgiveness, generosity, and love.

It is important to notice that in their turnaround they didn't simply take their children to church or teach them a few dos and don'ts. There is a misconception among Christians that if you bring your children to church, teach them right from wrong, and protect them from the sin of the world, they will magically grow into devoted Christians. While those are all very important steps, it's usually not enough. If the kids are grown yet not walking with the Lord, parents are sometimes left scratching their heads, feeling perplexed—and perplexed parents are becoming increasingly commonplace in the church these days.

Passing on a spiritual heritage to your children takes more than simply teaching God's Word; it takes *living out* God's Word. Fathers and mothers must become a picture of Jesus to their children. And that's what Dave and Stephanie did. They showed their kids, not just on Sundays but in everyday life, what it means to be a Christ follower. Jesus didn't only teach in the synagogue; He also served His disciples by washing their feet and offering them compassion, forgiveness, and sometimes correction.

As we saw earlier in Deuteronomy 5:9, the Lord says that He lays the sins of the parents upon their children; the entire family is affected—even children in the third and fourth generations after those who rejected Him.

This is a sobering truth, but it doesn't have to be that way. As we saw with Dave and Stephanie, and Mark and Jill, there is hope. The hope is found in Deuteronomy 5:10: He will lavish unfailing love for a thousand generations on those who love Him and obey His commands. This is a great blessing, and it gives us great hope!

In the chapters that follow, we will show you that even if you were raised in a damaged, imperfect home, your children are not predestined to grow up damaged themselves. We will show that you are not alone and that we, too, experienced flawed upbringings. You will learn how to recognize the three strands of a healthy legacy that can help you change direction with your own family as well as learn about specific tools to implement your own turnaround at home.

CHAPTER TWO

JACK'S HERITAGE

Nobody likes a stutterer. I know firsthand. Growing up with that embarrassing setback really took its toll on me. When you're a kid, just feeling different is bad enough, but when you've got a speech problem, it can be downright brutal. For me, a really great day was one when I didn't have to talk to anyone, but avoiding others was a project in itself. Eventually I would have to talk to someone—a teacher, another kid—but I hated it.

Nothing was worse than when I had to talk to my own dad. He was a rough and rugged farm boy from the plains of South Dakota and had been taught to be strong and independent. Prior to the end of World War II, my dad was so committed to the war effort that he lied about his age just to get into the Marine Corps. He was a hardworking man with the highest integrity—and to him, if you shook hands on a deal, then the deal was as good as done.

I am thankful for my dad's strong principles and that he taught us to keep our word and to respect authority. But weakness was not an acceptable trait in his eyes, and any perceived weakness was equally undesirable. So a kid like me, who was timid, reserved, and disengaged, would obviously have a tough go at it.

Here's the thing: boys look up to their fathers. I think that's just how God intended it to be. I don't think it's any accident that a boy seeks to mimic and emulate his dad. Because of this, fathers have an awesome responsibility. Just *being* a father sends a huge message to a son. Unfortunately for me, and perhaps you can relate, I had no sympathetic father to go to in times of need or trouble, and I felt I couldn't share with him the shame and embarrassment that stuttering had brought on. On the contrary—my father must have thought that the louder he yelled at me, the sooner my speech impediment would disappear. But that wasn't the case. To his amazement and my disappointment, nothing happened at all. I stuttered just as badly as I did before. I often heard the words, "Spit it out, will ya!" If just spitting it out would have done the trick, then I would have spit it out a long time before! So as I grew up, it became a daily effort to try to avoid my father. This, of course, created only a greater distance between us.

Looking back now, I believe my dad recognized that unless he did something to connect with me, I might end up as a lost cause. I remember as if it were yesterday.

"Jackson," he said to me, "get in the truck. I'm signing you up to play football."

I was nine years old and in the fourth grade. I couldn't believe my ears! Not that he was signing a fourth grader up for football, but that my dad wasn't yelling at me! He was actually talking to me. It was going to be just him and me in his truck, and he was going to sign me up for football! What could be better?

It was the late 1960s, and we lived in beautiful Orange County, California. Back then, full-contact football, at least for me, was the only way to spend every waking moment—and the Junior All American Football sports program allowed for just that. NFL heroes like Bart Starr, Joe Namath, and Dick Butkus were nearly gods. I was such a Green Bay Packers fan that every Sunday I would sit in front of the television, wearing my #15 Bart Starr jersey and my shiny green and yellow Packers helmet. I even went to bed with that helmet on my head! Football practice was almost every day of the week, and as it turned out, football was a great way to avoid conversation—an added bonus for a stutterer like me. We were expected to listen and obey, but there was an added perk: the helmet hid most of my face! Therefore, my identity was relegated to a number on a jersey. It felt great for a short period of time, but it didn't last long.

It was a perfect Southern California summer afternoon. Making my way across the field of a local school, I noticed a group of guys several years older—and bigger—than myself. These were notably the "tough guys." You know, the bullies. Recognizing the neighborhood stutterer alone and open game, they succeeded in knocking me to the ground. Considering that there were six of them, this was no great feat.

They then took delight in forcing me to talk and answer their questions just so they could hear me stutter. The ringleader, Eddie (can you believe that more than forty-five years later I can still remember his name?), thought it would be a good idea and somehow the crowning moment of his day if he could pull down his pants and urinate on my face, saying something to the effect of, "Maybe this will help you talk normal." In less than a second, whatever self-worth I thought I had gained in those weeks at football practice completely evaporated. I was so embarrassed, so full of shame, and so incredibly angry. The hurt I had been feeling inside grew exponentially. Little did I know that hurt feelings, if left unchecked, will turn into a deep-rooted bitterness that is destructive to healthy relationships. Again, having no one to turn to and no one to be my defender, I felt completely alone and vulnerable.

Parents, please hear me on this. When your children feel defenseless and unprotected, they may begin to turn inward and isolate themselves. That is not a good thing. As parents, we need to always see to it that we maintain an open door for our children to come to us at any time about anything. For me, in that moment, there was no one I had in my life to turn to.

Growing up, I had never been able to confide in my father, nor did I feel that he loved me. All I knew was that whatever I did, whatever mistakes I made, I'd better not involve him. By the time I was ten, I knew I could never live up to my father's expectations. I couldn't even figure out what goals he had for me. It was like a guessing game! Yet despite this, I never quit trying.

Over the years and through the experience of being a pastor, a father, and now a grandfather, I've learned that God designed us to be in the middle of a loving, nurturing family. Sadly I, like perhaps many of you reading this book, never seemed be good enough, even though I desperately longed to win my father's approval and acceptance.

Like any precocious child, I spent a lot of my time trying my best to figure out why I didn't seem to fit into my dad's world. I'd be lying if I said I'd never asked, "What's wrong with me, and why does it seem like my dad doesn't love me?" Those questions haunted me often as my ongoing struggle with stuttering just seemed to reinforce my insecurities. Eventually, however, I would come to understand why there was such distance between us.

My mother was of Portuguese descent but was born and raised in Oahu, Hawaii. Her mother died while giving birth to her, the youngest of five children. Her father, an alcoholic, decided he couldn't take care of them anymore, and so when my mother was four years old, he took her and her siblings to a Catholic orphanage and left them there. When she was sixteen, a Christian couple ended up taking her in as a foster child. She spoke mostly Pidgin English and an odd mixture of Hawaiian, Japanese, Portuguese, and Cantonese. My father, who was stationed in Hawaii, met my mother, and they were soon married. She was only seventeen years old and was looking for a way to start a new life. They moved into a small cottage, where she learned from other Hawaiian women how to cook and keep house. She gave birth to their first child while living in Hawaii, and then they moved to Coronado Island in San Diego, California, where both my older brother and I were born.

It might help to know that my mother's whole world revolved around the affairs of our home: she stayed home; cooked our breakfast, lunch, and dinner; cleaned (excessively); took care of us kids; and waited on my father. These were the only things she had in her life. She had no outside friends to speak of. She never went out to dinner. She never really went anywhere unless it involved us kids, at least as far as I can recall. She basically kept to herself, except when she spent time with a sister and a brother of hers who lived in our neighborhood.

I remember well one afternoon when I was a junior in high school. I had come home from school to grab something to eat before football practice and to catch an episode of my favorite television show—*Sea Hunt* with Lloyd Bridges. While I was watching it, I overheard my mom speaking to a neighbor in the kitchen, almost whispering. I could tell that their conversation was serious. My mom was emotional—I could hear it in her voice—and I'm certain she had no intention of ever telling me what was being discussed. In fact, to her dying day, she never knew I'd overheard what she had shared with the neighbor. Unbeknownst to the both of them, I was in the next room and within earshot of the revelation unfolding about a period of time in her life that included me.

Prior to the late 1950s, my mom and dad had one daughter and one son. Up to that point, their version of planned parenthood had gone off without a hitch. That is until the day my mother discovered she was pregnant with a third child.

Scared and a bit apprehensive about how her husband would cope with the news, she reluctantly braced herself to let him in on the "big surprise." But as she feared, his reaction was, shall we say, less than favorable.

The following days and weeks only seemed to widen the newly formed rift between them as my father repeatedly rejected the thought of them having another child. Eventually, as a way to avoid the unwanted pregnancy, he decided to use an opportunity to work far away in Alaska. This seemed to work for him, at least for a while.

I'm sure my mother must've felt alone and abandoned, and to be honest, over the years, I've often wondered if my father had secretly hoped she would just go and have an abortion.

On December 24, 1957, my mother was nearly full-term in her pregnancy with me. Although she had her ten-year-old daughter and her six-year-old son nearby, her husband was still away in Alaska. It was during the holiday season that loneliness and confusion began to overwhelm her.

As my mom continued to tell her story to the neighbor that afternoon, I learned that in her fear and desperation, she went into the kitchen and boiled a wire clothes hanger. She sterilized it in hopes of performing a "safe" abortion, then prepared the kitchen floor with a bedspread and towels. She then went about using the hanger. Unexpectedly, my aunt stopped by, interrupting the attempted abortion. My aunt unknowingly saved my life and possibly the life of my mother. My mother was admitted to Sharps Memorial Hospital that day, and a few weeks later, on January 15, 1958, I was, thankfully, granted a place in this world.

Nine months later, my father returned home to my mom and his three children.

A NEW FATHER

My mom may not have intended for me to hear that story, but I believe God did. In His awesome mercy, God knew that hearing the truth of my past was exactly what I needed. God used my situation and my upbringing to prepare my heart to someday respond to His message of grace.

On a Monday night in June 1977, I was planning on meeting up with some friends to go to a party in Newport Beach. Little did I know that I would turn into the parking lot of Calvary Chapel Costa Mesa. Frankly, I had no idea I was actually at a church. As I parked and got out of my car to see what was going on, I was amazed to see a couple of thousand young adults already inside the building. What in the world was happening here?

I sat wondering what would happen next. I had never been to church before, so this was a new experience for me. I had nothing to compare it to, so I thought to myself, *Man, if this is church, then why doesn't everybody go?* When the music stopped, a guy with long blond hair came out and said, "Let's turn in our Bibles …"

It was an amazing sound to hear all of those pages turning at the same time. Amazing—and a bit intimidating since I didn't have a Bible. The young man speaking that night was a bell-bottomed, sandal-wearing hippie named Greg Laurie. He began teaching from the book of Revelation. As he spoke, I was gripped by the truth I was hearing. I had never heard the Bible before, so every verse he quoted seemed to carry with it a strange urgency. As Greg continued to speak, he brought forth truth that I needed to hear. He talked about God, telling us that He was our heavenly Father and that we had full access to Him through Jesus Christ, His Son. I heard that God loved me enough to send His Son to cancel out my sins on the cross. Despite all my bitterness and anger, I learned that I couldn't earn God's love, as I had been trying so hard to do with my earthly father. I just had to believe in Him and trust Him to do and be who He said He was. When the time came to make that decision, I knew I had to go forward and repent, change my mind, and agree with God that I needed Him. Oh, how I needed Him to forgive me of my sins and to receive me into His care.

A PERFECT EXAMPLE

Immediately, God started changing me from the inside out. I studied God's Word as much as possible and attended Bible classes. I loved going and learning and still do! Through the power of the Word of God and by simply reading it, I was able to learn that by embracing my painful setbacks and the shame of my past, I could go from being a victim to being a victor, all because of the forgiveness I received from Him. Only God can take the ugly things and make something good out of them.

Words fail me now as I try to say how amazing it has been since that summer evening in 1977 when I first became a Christian.

Shortly after, I came across this passage that, over the years, has been a constant encouragement to me.

> Then the word of the LORD came to me, saying:
>
> "Before I formed you in the womb I knew you;
> Before you were born I sanctified you;
> I ordained you a prophet to the nations."
>
> Then said I:
>
> "Ah, Lord GOD!
> Behold, I cannot speak, for I am a youth." (Jer. 1:4–6)

His blessings and goodness continued, and within a few short years, I met and married my wife, Lisa. I now had a new life and a new purpose for living.

CHAPTER THREE

LISA'S HERITAGE

Unlike Jack, I grew up in a Christian home, although it might be more accurate to say that I grew up in two separate and distinct Christian homes—neither perfect, but both used by God to transform me into the wife, mother, and grandmother I am today.

I can remember only parts of my "first" Christian home, but I do remember the trauma I experienced from the untimely death of my mother. I was born the youngest of seven children, so many of my memories actually come from stories shared by my older siblings. A few are my own, however, including bits and pieces of the day my mother died. It was summertime, and I was five years old. My father woke us up, gathering us all in the living room. He seemed very sad, appearing as though he had been up all night. My older siblings were quite solemn and tearful as well. I remember a darkness that seemed to overtake the room.

"Jesus took Mommy to heaven," my father announced to all of us.

This was something I didn't like the sound of.

"Okay," I said. At least, it *seemed* as though it would be okay. *She'll be back*, I thought. *She's only gone on a trip. A trip to see Jesus!* I obviously had no clue or understanding of what my father was so delicately trying to say.

Even at her funeral, I was the only one smiling in all of the pictures. After all, why wouldn't I? I just didn't really understand why everyone was so upset. At one point, someone actually picked me up to look into her casket. They must have thought I needed to see what had happened to her. I'm sure it was out of a sincere desire to make me understand the reality of her death, but it certainly didn't work. I couldn't make the connection that the person lying there in that box was actually my mother and that she would never get up again.

My older siblings always told me that I was "tied to her apron strings." I guess I never wanted to leave her side—normally a good thing for any young child. But you can imagine that as the weeks went by, I grew increasingly upset. I missed my mommy, and I wanted her back! Everyone kept telling me she was in heaven, but I still didn't understand.

Several months earlier, with my mother's help, we had buried one of our cute, tiny green turtles that we kept as pets. As I struggled to understand the reality of my mother's death, I demanded to see what had happened to that little turtle. One of my older siblings even helped me dig it up. But when I saw what was left of the exhumed turtle, I began to realize that dead was forever. My mommy was gone for good. Soon I began having nightmares about the only terrible thing I had ever known: the abominable snowman from *Rudolph the Red-Nosed Reindeer*. In my dreams this "monster" came to my home and killed everyone in the house except for me. Then he went outside, and I watched as he drove a "For Sale" sign into the front lawn. My young life had been turned upside down.

But I certainly wasn't the only one. Death has a way of touching everyone a little bit differently. In my dad's case, the responsibility of raising seven children all by himself undoubtedly left him feeling stressed and confused. He was a very successful engineer, quiet, soft-spoken, and quite brilliant. He could fix anything and everything and loved to tinker with mechanical objects of every sort.

Unfortunately, as a young girl, I felt as though I never saw him much because he worked long hours. Even on the weekends when he was home, he was usually busy in the yard or working on something in the garage. He was never all that demonstrative with his love, so we never became as close as I would've wanted and certainly needed. In fact, I could probably count on one hand the times that he told me he loved me—and I so desperately wanted him to tell me and let me know that everything was going to be all right. The times he did say it, my eyes welled up with tears. To this day, I remember where I was and what I was doing when he told me because it meant so much to me. He, of course, never knew the effect his words had on me because I never let it show. I desperately wanted more of his love and attention but unfortunately never received it. At least not the way I needed it. I desired his love and care more than anything in the world.

My mother's death had been so unexpected that it had left all of us with a great deal of trauma and emotion to deal with. In my father's case, it was not long after her passing that he realized he would need help, and he would need it quickly.

A NEW MOTHER

Many of us love to play matchmaker, and in my father's situation, several people thought it was their duty to help him out, so he began going on some blind dates. Of course his friends all told these women his sad situation of him losing his wife so suddenly, yet they never relayed the little fact that he had seven children! But I actually enjoyed it when my dad went out with one particular woman because whenever they dated, she brought along her daughter to play with me and my older sister. This girl was only a year older than me and one year younger than my sister, and we all got along quite well. We quickly became friends, playing with our dolls and making up all sorts of games, so it didn't seem strange to me when, about a year after my mother died, my father asked a life-altering question while we all sat around the dining-room table one evening.

"How would you like a new mommy?" he asked, as if choosing a mother was as simple as choosing a new dress to wear.

I asked a simple question in response. "Does that mean Cindy will be my sister?"

"Yes."

Well, that's all my six-year-old ears needed to hear!

"Yay!" I exclaimed, clapping enthusiastically.

Of course, not everyone in the room was as excited. My older brothers and sisters, who were in their teens and twenties, thought their dad had lost his mind.

That day, the great pendulum of our family culture was about to swing from one extreme to another. The life we had been living in our home would never be the same. My easygoing mother was about to be replaced by someone altogether different, someone who favored strict adherence to rules. But truth be told, it may have been exactly what the doctor ordered. My new mother, my stepmother, was a very organized and levelheaded woman, one who laid the rules out right from the start.

This was all fine, at least for a while. But as time went on, the rules and strict order of the home became paramount—at least to me. Despite the respect I have for her now, my stepmother's regimented personality didn't exactly mesh well with my spirited personality, which I was told I inherited from my biological mother.

Before my mother died, I already had been handed the blessing of the sense and understanding of the love of God. Perhaps I learned it from my Sunday school classes, but I'm sure much of it must have come from my mother since we were together every day.

As I look back, I can see that my faith in God has always been very real to me. I never doubted His existence or that He was always there for me. Sometimes my growing faith demonstrated itself in somewhat humorous ways. For instance, there was the time when I was about four years old, standing on the edge of a neighbor's backyard pool. After hearing about the story of how Jesus and Peter walked on water, I thought that if I only had enough faith, I could do the same! So, closing my eyes, I said over and over, "I believe, I believe!"

Fortunately, my unwavering faith had a backup plan: I already knew how to swim!

While I had learned at least a portion of who God was from my mom, I would learn something else about God from my stepmother: the importance of discipline, obedience, and possessing sound doctrine.

Unfortunately, as I grew up, it seemed as though I was beginning to lose sight of the grace and love of God that had been extended to me in the past. It reminds me a little of the story *Les Misérables*, where Inspector Javert believed that law reigned supreme. It's not that I believe the law is wrong, because it obviously is not; after all, God Himself gave us the law for our protection and guidance. But law must be balanced with love—and that was something that, during my youth, I never felt from my stepmother. As a parent now myself, I can only imagine how difficult her task must've been as she took on seven stepchildren who were grieving the loss of their own mother.

When I was a young teenager, I reflected back on a time when I saw my biological mother and father sitting down together, drinking a beer. Having been under the tutelage of my stepmother for several years, I began to panic, fearing that my mother may have gone to hell because of drinking that beer.

I worried about this for years, until eventually, sometime after I was married, my aunt sent a card in the mail with a picture of my family. My mother had written all of our names and ages underneath the picture. I was two years old in the photograph and was sitting on her lap. But what was most significant to me was what my mom had written along the bottom.

> For God so loved the world that He gave His only begotten Son, that whosoever believes in Him should not perish but have everlasting life.

John 3:16. A message from my mom. A reminder of the grace and love of God.

My aunt wasn't even a Christian, but she'd sent it, saying, "I thought you kids would want this. I thought it was sweet." And then I knew it wasn't really a card from my aunt. It wasn't even from my mom. It was a note from the Lord, letting me know what I needed to remember—that my mom had believed in Him, and that drinking a beer was not going to revoke her salvation. Smiling, I thanked God for the peace that He gave me that day.

Days of Rebellion

Around that same time—and despite my stepmother's best intentions—I grew increasingly embittered by her strict adherence to the "rules." I was now in junior high, still desperately seeking the approval and affection of my father but rebelling against my stepmother's rigidity. I'm sure she may have been only trying to protect me, and much of what she did may have actually been in my best interests, but I just didn't respond well to *how* she did it.

My two sisters were one year and two years older than me. When we were younger, the age difference hadn't mattered so much, but by the time I reached the seventh grade, they were in the much more impressive ninth grade, doing much more exciting ninth-grade things. I guess to my stepmother, that meant danger for me. She didn't want me to grow up too fast, so I wasn't allowed to hang out with my older sisters' friends. This began to drive a wedge between my stepmother and me. I felt rejected, as though she hated me and wanted only to hurt me. I allowed that impression of her to grow into a deep bitterness, which turned into anger and then, I am sad to say, hatred.

It got so bad that eventually I wanted to hurt her in the same way she had hurt me. I felt so unloved by her that I wanted to get even somehow. I was a foolish teenager who was hurting emotionally. In my rebellion, I entered the party scene, showing up where I knew I shouldn't be, doing things I knew I shouldn't be doing. I was constantly feeling guilt and shame. Often I would come home, cry, and open my Bible to the book of Psalms. There I would read of David's persecution and his cry to the Lord for help. In some naive way, I thought David and I were in the same boat! He was being persecuted, and so was I!

I would then ask God to forgive me, for I knew very well the difference between right and wrong. I justified my actions by saying it was all her fault. She was hurting me, so I would hurt her. I actually reasoned with God by telling Him that He and I were okay, and not to worry about all this stuff because this was between me and her!

By the beginning of my senior year, however, I took things too far. At the grocery store where I worked, there was a cute German guy about three years older than me. He was a quiet guy who kept to himself, so I made it my mission to get him to open up. Well, it worked, and it wasn't long before we were dating, expressly against my stepmother's rules about dating older guys. Within a few months I had crossed a line that I never should have crossed. I didn't even really like the guy that much—after all, I was dating him only to get back at my stepmother. Or so I thought.

A couple of months later my dad found out about our relationship, and it all came to a screeching halt. He had a long talk with this guy, and the outcome was not a good one. To my shock, this young man had really become fond of me and had no idea that this foolish girl had one mission in her life: to hurt her stepmother. He was devastated. I, however, wasn't all that concerned. Not about him, anyway.

The only concern I had at that moment was the look on my father's face—one I will never forget. There was great disappointment and anger in his eyes, and it broke me instantly. I was distraught beyond belief. I had let down the one person from whom I had craved only approval and love. How could I have been so foolish? I set out to hurt one (my stepmother) and ended up hurting another (my father). Isn't that what sin so often does? We end up hurting the ones we never intended to hurt.

I had justified my rebellion by blaming someone else. But in the end, I ultimately hurt my relationship with both my earthly dad and my heavenly Father.

Just the look on my dad's face was the beginning of the end of my rebellion. But our God always has a plan.

TURNING IT AROUND

When I first met Jack, several months later, I was ready for a change. A big change! I knew my walk with the Lord wasn't strong, but I really didn't know what to do to make things any better. I didn't have any good Christian friends, so I just went to church and tried to do the best I could.

Jack had been a Christian for only about ten months, struggling with the same problem: no Christian friends. He had been going to church alone at Calvary Chapel Costa Mesa but hadn't connected with anyone. So on our first date he took me to a church service there on a Monday night. I was amazed to see a very large group of young people who were all holding Bibles, waiting in line to go into church!

I had never seen this before, as I had grown up faithfully attending a small Baptist church. I loved my church and have to this day many fond memories of my time there, but I didn't really understand how to study the Bible and make it applicable to my everyday life. From the very first night I attended the service at Calvary Chapel, I started learning and being taught in a way that was new and exciting. My ears were open to hear all that the Lord desired to do in my life. Maybe it was just because I was finally ready to listen and obey. I had been heading in the wrong direction for several years, had lost the respect and trust of my parents, and was now willing and ready to let the Lord put my life back together and rebuild it with a solid and proper foundation.

Jack and I started attending services every chance we could. We loved studying and hearing the Word of God! We were so excited that we both had found someone who desired and loved the same thing. We soon married (I was nineteen years old), and we began going to church at Calvary Chapel almost every night of the week, taking as many classes as possible. Who would've known that, years later, the Lord would use those special, instructive years as preparation for the ministry?

From my teen years on, I had always known what it was that I wanted to do with my life: be a mom. Not just any mom, mind you, but the best mom. I was going to do things differently from what I had seen. I had felt so lost growing up, so unloved, that I thought the best way to fix all that was to pour into my own children the love that I had so desperately wanted.

Funny thing is, after I had our first child and started raising her to love Jesus, I found that all those "stifling" rules my stepmother had enforced upon me were the very principles that I wanted to teach my daughter, too. They were all biblically based values that are so very important to know and obey. I would enforce them, of course, but I also realized that I needed to show the unfailing *love* of the Father as well. There needed to be a balance between the two, because that's how our heavenly Father treats us.

I desperately wanted something different for my children, and yet here Jack and I were, two very imperfect people with vastly different upbringings, hoping to turn things around with our own family. How could we possibly do this? How could we raise our kids right when neither one of us had received a strong family heritage ourselves? What kind of legacy would we be able to give to our children?

It's sobering to think of trying to accomplish such a thing without any guidance or encouragement. And don't get me wrong—by no means did we do a perfect job, though we did what we thought was best at the time. After that first baby came along, I realized that I thought I knew what to do to be a great mom, but I was fully unaware of how really unequipped I was.

Fortunately, about that time a new ministry started up called Focus on the Family with Dr. James Dobson. I listened almost every day to his radio program and then tried to put into practice all that I learned. What a lifesaver he was for me as a young mom!

As you trust the Lord to help you, you will find that God equips you to handle the job. We did raise our children in the ways of the Lord, although not perfectly. We knew that God had a better way and that He had brought us together for a purpose, but it's certainly not always easy. The Lord has given us two beautiful daughters, who are now grown and have the privilege of instilling within their children a godly legacy. And they are, prayerfully, doing a better job at it than we did!

We wanted to be a part of writing this book because of the encouragement we can give you that you can learn from what has happened in your own past—the good, the bad, and the ugly—and make changes necessary to build a strong legacy and have a Christ-centered home. You yourself can be a picture of Jesus to your children, demonstrating the balance of His unconditional love with the understanding of obeying His purposeful commands. God has a plan, and He gives us the boundaries in which we are to live—not for our hurt, as I once believed, but ultimately for our good.

CHAPTER FOUR

YOUR HERITAGE

Every family has a heritage—a legacy passed from one generation to the next. For some, that legacy might include simple family traditions such as saying a prayer before dinner, gathering for a celebration/holiday meal, or going Christmas caroling through the neighborhood. For others that legacy might be evenings filled with demeaning one another with hurtful, angry words, or perhaps saying nothing at all while staring at yet another mind-numbing television program. It might even entail finding a way to spend every waking moment as far from your family as you possibly can.

If you're like many parents, you might not be putting a lot of thought into your heritage. We would like to encourage you to take the time now to consider the impact that it has not only on your life but also on the lives of those you love. After all, understanding your own heritage is foundational to giving your children something better than you received.

So what exactly is a heritage, and how will it impact your own family? Let's start with some basics.

> A **heritage** is the spiritual, emotional, and social
> legacy that is passed from parent to child, either
> for good or for bad.

Every parent should ask himself or herself this question: How might the heritage I received affect the heritage I am giving my children?

Lisa and I came from two very different backgrounds, yet we were both dogmatic about our family time. Giving thanks and eating meals together became a priority, as did praying individually with

our children before bedtime (even through the teen years) and bringing them up to know the difference between right and wrong from
a biblical worldview. For us, God became a constant conversation
with our children, whether it was looking at bugs or trying to make
a decision about life's next chapter.

On the flip side, we've learned—even during the writing of this
very book—that Lisa and I didn't always show or express enough
compassion and sympathy toward our children as they dealt with
fears and insecurities. We've spoken to them and discovered that our
own emotionally unsupportive homes trickled down into their lives
as well. The heritage we left, while better than what we had received,
still left room for great improvement!

Every heritage has three distinct yet interrelated parts: the
spiritual, the emotional, and the social. As Solomon pointed out in
Ecclesiastes 4:12, "A cord of three strands is not quickly broken"
(HCSB). Therefore, the three interwoven components of a heritage are
at their strongest when bound together. Separate or isolated cords
provide only a little strength at best, and in truth, nothing by itself
can truly be strong. The heritage cord, then, is like a rope tying a
person to his or her past.

Predictably, when life tosses us around like a dinghy in a storm,
a strong heritage is something secure to hold on to. If the heritage
hasn't been weakened or tossed aside entirely, it will serve as an
anchor, keeping you from drifting further away from who you've
been designed to be. And when the time comes for you, as the parent, to hand this cord over to your children, you will empower them
to set sail on their own course. Yet they will always be linked to the
identity and direction you set for them.

PARTS OF ONE PACKAGE

We must be careful, because it is unwise to overemphasize one aspect of a strong heritage at the expense of the other two. When one strand is weak, the entire cord suffers. Our emotional, social, and spiritual dimensions are part of a complete package: one heavily influencing the other two. Even so, it is helpful to identify the unique dynamic each component brings. Because of this, we will explore their impact and importance in greater depth separately in the chapters that follow.

For now, let's briefly touch upon the three strands.

THE SPIRITUAL

As we saw with my own (Jack's) heritage, many homes totally neglect the spiritual element of the threefold cord, even though it is vital. When I was growing up, there was no awareness of God or of who defined absolute right or wrong. In situations like mine, moral relativism often becomes the norm, leaving children to figure out for themselves what they believe and what they do not believe. Parents often unintentionally fail to offer their children a healthy spiritual basis for life. Either they have no spiritual understanding themselves, or they incorrectly assume that their kids will *just get it* by osmosis even if their parents aren't actively living out their faith.

In a healthy Christian home, parents embody the nurturing love and protective security of our heavenly Father. By contrast, in a broken or troubled home, children might perceive God as absent, distant, condemning, or overly demanding. Because we are all spiritual beings who need spiritual understanding and expression, in the absence of absolute truth we find a poor replacement to fill the void. Consider what Paul said to those in Athens:

> Men of Athens, I observe that you are very religious in all respects. For while I was passing through and examining the objects of your worship, I also found an altar with this inscription, "TO AN UNKNOWN GOD." Therefore what you worship in ignorance, this I proclaim to you. (Acts 17:22–23 NASB)

I was much like those men in Athens; I had been raised with no spiritual training as a child. So when I finally came to know Christ, my first reaction was to fashion God into someone much like my own father. I would spend each morning trying to *earn* God's love for that day by making myself pray for hours at a time. I would rise at four o'clock in the morning and start praying, only to fall asleep shortly thereafter. In guilt and desperation, I soon resorted to stripping naked and climbing into a cold, dry bathtub in a monastic effort to stay awake. I didn't want to disappoint my Father in heaven. I believed that He demanded my strict adherence in order to maintain our relationship—something that was sadly normal in my relationship with my earthly father. I wrongly believed that I had to earn my heavenly Father's love in the same way I had thought I could earn my earthly father's love.

Like many others, I had no godly model. Frankly, I had received no spiritual legacy at all. The result? I was much like the Athenians, having a skewed understanding of who or what God was. I ended up worshipping an "unknown god" with characteristics that had little similarity to the one true God of Scripture. Lisa, too, had to overcome her childhood perceptions of God as seen through the lens of a distorted spiritual legacy.

Every one of us yearns for spiritual sustenance and spiritual purpose. Even the people of ancient Greece sought after truth, often finding glimpses of it in pagan religions. But the clear, beautiful, compelling picture of the one true God was quickly drowned out by the loud but hollow sounds of a false worldview.

It might be good to say at this point that Lisa and I strongly advocate biblical Christianity as the one true and proper foundation upon which to build a spiritual heritage. Just like the apostle Paul speaking to the men of Athens, we hope to point those seeking truth to the One who called Himself the way, the truth, and the life.

THE EMOTIONAL

Each of us is an emotional reflection of the environment in which we were raised. For better or for worse, our emotional environment has a profound impact upon our emotional well-being as adults. For example, those reared in an atmosphere of love and acceptance tend to be more secure than those raised in a critical, distant family. Likewise, if you came from a home in which affection was rarely demonstrated, you may find expressing your love more difficult than those from a family of huggers.

In *When Anger Hits Home*, Gary Oliver and H. Norman Wright explain how parents influence a child's emotional legacy:

One of the most important factors is our home environment. Some of us grew up in homes [where] emotions were not modeled or discussed. The few emotions that were expressed were kept behind closed doors.... Others grew up in homes where emotional expression was punished and emotional repression was reinforced. Children raised in this environment either consciously or unconsciously told themselves that it wasn't safe to feel. [With anger,] some adults had a parent who was a silent sulker. Others had a parent who played the martyr. Yet others had parents who were screamers or raging hulks.... No matter what the style, how you saw your parents handling their anger influenced how you handle your anger now. Your past shapes your present handling of emotions.[1]

Regardless of your upbringing, you *can* overcome the negative. But you must first be able to recognize it and then weed out the unhealthy from the healthy. In chapter 6 we will examine the impact of the emotional legacy you may have been given, as well as the importance of surrounding your own children with love and security.

THE SOCIAL

Much like our emotional heritage, how we *relate* to others as adults often grows out of how social issues were handled in the home. Our parents, for example, exemplify how to treat (or how *not* to treat) a husband or a wife. With our siblings, we practice the skills of sharing and caring—and sometimes fighting. We spend our formative years with our families, eating meals together (or not), playing games together (or not), taking vacations together (or not), and talking together (you guessed it—or not).

Hopefully we learn something about all levels of human relationships in the process through both laughter and pain. Those early experiences leave their mark on who we are and how we interact with others.

GOOD OR BAD

Consider the family of Jonathan Edwards, the famous eighteenth-century preacher and theologian and one of America's greatest intellectuals. It is interesting to examine what kind of heritage he received and what kind of legacy he left behind.

Jonathan's father was a minister, and his mother the daughter of a clergyman. Among their descendants into the late twentieth century were fourteen college presidents, more than a hundred college professors, more than a hundred lawyers, thirty judges, and sixty physicians! The family also has given us more than a hundred clergymen, missionaries, and theology professors and about sixty authors. Jonathan himself was the grandfather of the third vice president of the United States!

Contrast the rich heritage and impact of the Edwards' line with the influence of the Jukes family. It has been estimated that this family has cost the state of New York millions of dollars over the years. Since the eighteenth century, the Jukes have produced three hundred professional paupers, sixty thieves, and a hundred and thirty convicted criminals. Fifty-five descendants were victims of sexual obsession and only twenty ever learned a trade (and ten of those learned it in a state prison). Sadly, this family produced at least seven murderers.

Is there any question that prior generations can have a direct influence over our own life patterns? But what legacy will we leave behind? A family rich with success, or one plagued with dysfunction?

HOPE FOR THE FUTURE

Some of us, like Jonathan Edwards, have been blessed to receive a strong heritage. We received a solid cord placed directly into our hands, a cord made up of healthy spiritual, emotional, and social strands. Many more of us, however, have received a weakened cord, where one or more of those strands came to us damaged or missing altogether. Often despite their best intentions, our parents failed to protect a positive heritage, leaving us unprepared for what would come our way. Some have suffered from indifference and neglect, others from abuse, whether physical, sexual, or verbal.

Many of you will identify with me (Jack), reared in a home where I never felt the love of my father, or perhaps Dave from chapter 1, who acquired his hedonistic lifestyle from his divorced parents. But let this serve as an encouragement that one weak strand doesn't have to spell ruin for passing on a strong heritage. Though neither Dave nor I received a good heritage, we were both determined to give one nonetheless. And that resolve was the first step toward restoring the damaged cord we received.

The same can be true for you.

Understanding the impact of your heritage is vital to living an effective and meaningful life. It can give you a new perspective on your past, a calm confidence in the present, and a meaningful sense of vision for your future.

Whether you received a wonderful heritage and are determined to pass it along to your own children or you grew up in a home filled with anger, disharmony, or abuse, we will offer some practical tools for creating a heritage for your children. You will learn to glean from the good of your upbringing while letting go of the painful past, enabling you to embrace the understanding of God's grace and power for your own life.

BREAKING THE CYCLE

In truth, none of us were handed a *perfect* heritage. Because of the sinful, depraved nature of humanity, we have all received a mix of good and bad. Our parents, limited by their own weaknesses and learning through trial and error, did not always offer what was needed. Our children, for example, had what some would consider a fortunate break, being raised in a pastor's home. But they will tell you today that life in the fishbowl was anything but a picnic. They were constantly held to a different standard by those around them, and their mother and I often expected more than we should have. They, like all of us, received both good and bad.

What about *your* heritage? Perhaps you received a good emotional legacy, while the spiritual and social elements of your heritage were weak. Or you may have received a positive spiritual legacy, but your emotional heritage left much to be desired. Do the negative, weak strands in your cord make it difficult to find the strength in the positive? We will always be tempted to throw the baby out with the bathwater when we unnecessarily focus on the negative rather than the positive. *A word to the wise:* we need to be careful that we aren't too quick to reject the entire inheritance we were given because of the unpleasant parts.

In the process of closing off the pain, we may end up closing off our link to the past. Such an unhealthy response undermines our sense of identity and stifles our ability to grow. Rejecting what we've been handed is not the solution. Rather, we should seek to understand it and build upon it. We must identify and keep the good, while sorting out and replacing the bad.

Here are five people who are trying to do just that. Dedicated to passing on their heritage, they are struggling because of a weakened cord received from their parents. Some have made a turnaround. Others have not. All of them offer a snapshot into how what we received impacts what we will give to the next generation.

CATHY'S STORY

Cathy, twenty-nine and married, rejected the inheritance from her parents and had no desire to build and pass on that heritage to her children. Now, as her children are growing, she has begun to realize that they are suffering from the fallout of her own disillusioned past.

Cathy's parents had been ministers, but they found the demands of ministry life too much; they gave up on their dream of reaching the world with the good news of the gospel and resigned the commission. They had spent much time with Cathy in her early years, sharing and living their values, and laying the foundation for a strong heritage. But the disappointment and exhaustion they experienced after they left their ministry call began to drive the husband and wife apart. Within a matter of months, they began living separate lives. They rarely spoke to each other, and both struggled with the uncertainties of the future.

Watching from the sidelines, Cathy was numbed by hurt. The fragile sense of identity she had been building began to fade right in front of her. The thought plagued her mind: *Mom and Dad don't really love each other. Maybe they never really loved me either.*

Her parents finally divorced, and her brothers and sister scattered, carrying their own crop of bitterness with them. After having been handed a good heritage early on, Cathy watched her parents undermine what she had received. What at one time made perfect sense to her—what at one time made her comfortable—had now shaken her at her foundation. Cathy began questioning every spiritual, emotional, and social aspect of the heritage they wanted to give her.

As a result, the pendulum swung from one extreme to the other in all three areas. *Before* the collapse of her parents' marriage, she had been a very strong, good-humored, levelheaded young woman. She could handle practically any emotional strain.

Afterward, she would fly off at the slightest challenge to her opinion. She seemed always on the edge of an angry outburst or else on the verge of tears.

"Before the divorce, I enjoyed the warmth of a close-knit family and strong friendships," Cathy once said with regret in her voice. "Afterward, I went so far as to call any relative who dared to show that they cared, ordering them to stay out of my life. Having alienated them all, I began entering into unhealthy relationships." She dated abusive boyfriends and hung out with negative and irreverent girlfriends. She looked to these people for acceptance, but they served only to undermine her identity further.

Her spiritual life went from a vital source of joy to a haunting source of bitterness. "I began to see God as a bully, a mean-spirited ruler without a real heart. A deity, yes, but a deity who doesn't much care about me." Yet down deep, she wanted more. She scurried from church to church, trying to find the God she needed, while rejecting the God she had known.

PAUL AND JOANN: THE BLENDED FAMILY

Paul is a tall, balding fellow with a broad vocabulary and a keen mind. Joann, approaching middle age, is an attractive woman and a bottom-line person. When talking to Joann, you sense the need to get to the point, cut to the chase, and skip the gory details.

Both previously married with children, Paul and Joann are trying to create a heritage for their blended family. They have turned to their pastor to give them a gut-level understanding of what they should do with their children. They don't blame their ex-mates for their failed marriages. But they are determined to make *this* marriage strong and are committed to creating a lasting heritage for their children.

Creating harmony in a blended family is a major feat for anyone. They each have a daughter from their first marriages, and now they have one daughter and one son from this union as well. Joann's daughter from her first marriage is now pregnant out of wedlock and has no plans to marry the father. Paul's daughter is deeply involved in the drug culture. She lives on the streets and is a constant threat to the safety of Paul's present family. Neither Paul nor Joann was handed a decent heritage, but they want desperately to begin one for their kids. They have questions:

> "Is it possible?"
> "Is it too late for us?"
> "Are we wasting our time even trying?"
> "How difficult will it be?"
> "Does this heritage thing really work?"

They will learn that it is possible, that it's rarely too late, and, yes, that "this heritage thing" has lasting rewards that do work and are biblical.

MEET BILLY

Most people who meet Billy would say, "He'll never make it." Let's look at a list of his experiences and let them speak for themselves:

> He was born to a couple that did not want him.
> His dad was a drug user and dealer.
> His mother knew nothing but the streets.
> From childhood, he was a drug user himself.
> He used street language and manners.
> He was very angry and it showed in his fists.

When Billy finally married, his anger didn't just magically disappear. His rage continued, directed now toward his wife and children. He beat his wife and became a pathological liar. Though he started school, intending to help the family and himself by getting a better job, he eventually dropped out. Later he tried to drop out of life as well with an overdose of amphetamines.

Billy has two children, both boys. Thanks to encountering the principles outlined in this book he now has one desire. A good desire. "I want to put this marriage back together and begin building a strong heritage for my kids."

It *is* possible.

OLIVIA'S INHERITANCE

She came into the world because of the abuse of her father. One night a drunken Joe walked into the house and ordered his wife to the bedroom. "Get upstairs and do your wifely duty!" He proceeded to empty his passions while tears fell down her face. Olivia was conceived at that moment.

Olivia's mother, devastated by the years of Joe's abuse and neglect and now carrying a child conceived in pain, secretly asked her own mother for help. She packed up the five kids and escaped from years of abuse and disrespect. The divorce was final about the same time Olivia was born. Her mom worked hard to raise six children alone. A full-time job and night school kept her away most of the time, so Olivia more or less raised herself. She had no one to advise her on right and wrong, no one to hold her when she was hurting, no one to cheer her accomplishments, no one to teach her about boys, no one to model healthy family living.

The other parents on the street didn't want their children playing with Olivia or her siblings because they were ill-kept and ill-mannered. And so heartache, loneliness, and rejection became Olivia's inheritance.

But that was then. Olivia grew up to become Olivia Bruner, wife of our coauthor and friend Kurt. Today, Olivia is building a wonderful heritage of love for her own family. She has broken the cycle of pain from her past and is launching a new era in her home. How did she make such a dramatic transition in life? By learning how to give and receive an inheritance of love. We will tell you more of her story later. Hers is a story of hope. Hers is a story of how a person can give what she did not receive.

Olivia's story demonstrates the powerful impact of an "extended heritage," where other adults extend their heritage to children outside their own family. Her experience serves as a model for much of what we have learned and will share about building a heritage. Remember our definition of the word *heritage*: the emotional, spiritual, and social legacy that is passed from parent to child ... good or bad.

As you evaluate your own experience and family heritage, do you like what you see? If so, have you identified a plan of action for passing that tradition on to others? If not, are you ready to rise above the cycle of hurt and begin a new tradition for yourself and your family? The rest of this book will help you through that process. Let's begin by taking a closer look at what makes a heritage good or bad.

CHAPTER FIVE

YOUR SPIRITUAL LEGACY

In the previous chapter we saw that every heritage includes spiritual, emotional, and social components. It's critical that we clearly understand the meaning and impact of each. Once again, however, the three are so heavily intertwined that we hesitate to address them independently. The last thing we want to do is reinforce the notion that they can be wholly separated from one another. One may heavily influence the other two, but none stands alone when it comes to giving and receiving a solid heritage.

Still, there is value in taking a look at the unique role each has in defining who we are and how we got that way. Let's begin by inspecting the spiritual.

Sometimes the spiritual seems the least tangible of the three. Unlike the emotional or social strands of the heritage, the effects of spiritual matters on your child's behavior aren't always visible. Spiritual progress is often more difficult to observe and measure. Yet it is first and foremost of the three because of its eternal consequences. In fact, your child's sense of identity and purpose depends largely upon spiritual understanding and connection. We *are* spiritual beings. First Thessalonians 5:23 refers to us as threefold creatures: body, soul, and *spirit*. No heritage is complete or healthy unless it has been built upon a biblical, spiritual foundation.

DEFINITION

The goal of a strong spiritual legacy is to give the child a solid foundation for living with confidence in the unseen realities of the spiritual life. In terms of how we create such a legacy, here is our first definition:

> A **spiritual legacy** is the process whereby parents
> model and reinforce the unseen realities of the
> spiritual life.

Perhaps the most significant part of our definition is that *parents model.* This goes beyond just instruction and/or knowledge and into the actual living out of spiritual truths. In many ways, this helps us determine what a spiritual legacy *is not.*

A spiritual legacy is not …

Church attendance. Don't get us wrong. Involvement in a local body will often strengthen the cord. But too frequently parents rely on someone else to teach their children spiritual truths. Consider Stephanie from chapter 1. She was raised in a family that actively attended church yet just as actively ignored its teachings, leaving her spiritually confused.

Bible reading. Scriptural principles are a vital part of spiritual perspective, but reading about scriptural principles pales in comparison to actually *seeing* them lived out. Perhaps you've heard it said: "Preach the gospel at all times. When necessary, use words." There are a great many intellectuals in the world who have read the entire Bible yet have rejected the gospel message it embodies. Clearly, reading Scripture, while important, is not enough, whereas teaching the gospel to our children is easier when we actually live like we believe it!

Formal religious instruction. It's true that the absence of religious instruction may cause a major void in one's worldview. But it's also true that religious instruction apart from practical application is of little value. It is unlikely that knowing the four spiritual laws or the names of all the kings of Judah will be of much aid when it is time to help a child deal with the loss of a close family member. Only a practical, working knowledge of the Bible can bring comfort at such times.

All of these things contribute to a spiritual legacy, yet none of them define it.

A spiritual legacy—like our emotional and social legacies—is influenced far more by a parent's actions and attitudes than by the roles and rules of institutions or by repetitious religious practices. We can see this clearly in three elements of our second definition of a legacy:

> **legacy**: something resulting from, and left behind
> by, an action, event, or person.[1]

In other words, a legacy is more what we do than what we say. By our *actions*, we model the spiritual elements in our lives for our world—and our children—to see.

Also, notice in the first definition that a spiritual legacy is a process, not just an event. A baby dedication ceremony, for example, is only a starting point in the life of that little baby. His parents did not give him a legacy that day. The legacy comes through years of consistent sacrificial and committed effort. The dedication ceremony takes on meaning not in and of itself, but through all the hard work that follows. The "event" doesn't "result in something." Instead, it is a declaration of intent. Because of this, we don't really earn the right to celebrate a legacy until we have paid the price to build one.

Next, parents model and reinforce a spiritual legacy. Spiritual realities are more *caught* than *taught*; the child observes the parents and sees the truth of the spiritual life in action. Indeed, a strong spiritual legacy is modeled (an act of love), not mandated (an act of law). It occurs in the routine moments of life and is transferred over dinner-table conversations, etc. A solid spiritual legacy is more about the daily grind than it is about weekly worship. Our children need to observe the spiritual life as part of normal living rather than the exclusive domain of saintly grandmothers and professional theologians.

We cannot necessarily *teach* our children good character traits and what it means to be a person of sound integrity. This is something that they must see *demonstrated* in our behavior. For example, all of us would like our children to be honest. But if your friend just got her hair cut or bought a new outfit and your child hears you tell her you like it while at home you say the opposite, are you teaching your child truthfulness? Children pick up on these inconsistencies almost immediately. The same is true for all character qualities you would like to see in your children. I'm reminded of this humorous anonymous quote: "Children are natural mimics who act like their parents despite every effort to teach them good manners."

Finally, a strong spiritual legacy prepares our children to clearly recognize the unseen realities of the spiritual life. Each of us enters this world with an intuitive awareness that reality is more than the external. Foundational principles govern our existence and are part of the spiritual life. These principles address such questions as the following:

Who is God?

What is truth?

Who are we in relation to God?

Who is Jesus? Why did He die on a cross? Did He really rise from the grave?

Is the devil real? What are his weapons?

Is there a heaven? Is there a hell?

Unfortunately, because these principles are unseen and uncomfortable for many, some parents mistakenly neglect this vital aspect of passing a spiritual heritage on to their children. We've all heard the comments:

"I'll let my children decide for themselves when they get older."

"I don't want to be a hypocrite."

"I hated all that church stuff growing up, so I'm not going to force it on my kids."

Such comments highlight a fundamental misunderstanding of spiritual realities in our culture. We have compartmentalized our spirituality and extracted it from the rest of life. This is tragic and dangerous. Unseen realities influence our daily decisions. When we fail to clarify and reinforce them, we rob our children of a critical element in decision making as well as of a vital part of their heritage.

I personally believe that America today is suffering from an absence of real biblical Christianity. Sadly, many have relegated their spiritual experience to a sixty- to ninety-minute event on Sunday morning. Until we take Christianity seriously and begin to understand that it is a total commitment and life change for followers of Jesus Christ, we will continue to see our nation's spiritual health decline. Spiritual growth should take place in the home on a daily basis, complemented by our local church gatherings on the weekend; one should not exclude the other.

The Power of the Unseen

Despite her generally strong spiritual upbringing, my wife, Lisa, still struggled in her teen years with the unseen realities of a God she misunderstood. If you recall, from her youth Lisa had a fleeting memory of her biological mother having a beer. As a result, she feared for her mother's salvation. Her perception of who God was and how He administered judgment was directly impacted by her stepmother's emphasis on rules and the legalistic thinking that emphasis brought upon her. Until you understand who God is as revealed in Scripture and through the truth revealed in Jesus Christ, you will have a wrong or incomplete view of who He really is. How you perceive God may be more a reflection of the way you were parented than of the truth of who He is as He is revealed in Scripture.

Consider Billy, the second-generation drug and wife abuser described in the previous chapter. The spiritual part of his heritage seemed nonexistent. Intensely angry and given to cursing anything that upset him, Billy's greatest handicap was his inability to see anything from a spiritual standpoint.

His parents had made no effort to suggest that there was a loving God. As a result, his image of God was disfigured and his view of Scripture deformed; he regarded all "religious" people as "weak-minded crutch leaners."

For Billy, the spiritual world was indeed alien territory. No wonder his life was in tremendous need of major repair. He could not see the foundational *unseen* realities of life, which can be observed only by having a solid spiritual legacy. Able to see only the *seen* realities of life, he limped along without even realizing he had a serious handicap.

Without a solid foundation of scriptural truth to draw from, we are left wandering through life without any clear direction or sense of real purpose. We are left to fall into the traps laid out by the father of lies himself, Satan.

These foundational yet unseen realities are the basis for everything else we do: how we treat others, how we demonstrate love to our children, our ability to forgive, and even our careers. As you'll see in the following two chapters, the unseen realities of a strong or weak spiritual legacy exert an observable force upon the emotional and social strands of our heritage. When you are facing emotional turmoil, having a strong spiritual understanding of God's unfathomable love can help you endure and overcome any situation. Remember this:

> Yet in all these things we are more than conquerors through Him who loved us. (Rom. 8:37)

Similarly, being raised in a home that lives out Jesus's servant heart directly influences how you view and respect others around you.

Evaluating Your Own Spiritual Legacy

Before we can effectively develop a strategy for passing a good heritage on to our children, it is critical that we each examine the heritage we were given. The Spiritual Legacy Evaluation that concludes this chapter can help you measure the heritage you have received.

First, let's briefly highlight some of the characteristics of a good and bad spiritual legacy.

Traits of a Good Spiritual Legacy

Perhaps the most important characteristic of a good spiritual legacy is that it gives one *a foundation for understanding how God works in one's life.* In contrast, a bad spiritual legacy will cause someone to interpret spirituality as luck, fate, self, or perhaps another god such as money, pleasure, people, or some other belief system. It should be noted that when we speak of spirituality, we mean a biblically based spirituality that should not be confused with the spirituality of this world—for example, Eastern mysticism, the cults, New Age beliefs, or any other aberrant faith movement.

A second characteristic is *balance.* Some people are so heavenly minded they isolate themselves from those who need to hear spiritual truths. In other words, they are no earthly good. For fear of being tainted, they make themselves untouchable rather than being like Jesus, who went after those who needed the love He had to give. Others are so focused on the materialism and goods of this world that they lose track of what is truly important in life. Acting as a plumb line, a good spiritual legacy shows us a balance between these two extremes.

A third characteristic is *genuineness in our dealings.* This applies to how our parents presented the spiritual component to us. Some of us may have understood Christianity as something acknowledged only at

Christmas and Easter rather than as a dynamic part of family living. Others have lived under the heavy weight of rules and regulations that were burdensome when it came to real life. In both cases, the child receives an inadequate or damaged spiritual legacy from the parents.

For example, that was the foremost problem for a friend named Jim, whose parents did not pass on a healthy spiritual legacy. They weren't exactly atheist or agnostic, yet the big family Bible resting on the coffee table was little more than a decorative prop. They did not use the Bible as a source of absolute, reliable truth. And Jim and his siblings knew it.

LEADING LEGACY INDICATORS

Below is a list summarizing the Leading Legacy Indicators for the spiritual dimension of your personal legacy. The indicators highlight some of the key differences between a good and bad spiritual legacy. It should be noted that the list states the extremes. Obviously, most of us experienced something in between the two. But it is helpful, nonetheless, as a tool for comparative evaluation. When reading through, you might recognize some of these indicators from your own upbringing or perhaps even in how you are raising your children today.

A STRONG SPIRITUAL LEGACY ...

- Acknowledges and reinforces spiritual realities.
- Views God as a personal, caring Being who is to be both loved and respected.

- Makes spiritual activities a priority in life (church attendance, prayer, Scripture reading, serving, etc.).
- Talks about spiritual issues as a means of reinforcing spiritual commitments.
- Clarifies timeless truth and right from wrong.
- Incorporates spiritual principles into everyday living.

A WEAK SPIRITUAL LEGACY ...

- Undermines or ignores spiritual realities.
- Represents God as an impersonal being.
- Never or rarely participates in spiritual activities.
- Has few spiritual discussions of a constructive nature.
- Confuses absolutes and upholds relativism.
- Separates the spiritual from the practical.

Again, this list is by no means comprehensive. It does, however, identify some of the key areas that affect a spiritual legacy.

SPIRITUAL LEGACY EVALUATION

Answer each question by circling the number that best reflects the legacy you have received from your parents; then add together to find your total score.

1. To what degree were spiritual principles incorporated into daily family life?

    1 – Never

    2 – Rarely

    3 – Sometimes

    4 – Frequently

    5 – Almost always

    6 – Consistently

2. Which word captures the tone of how you learned to view and relate to God?

    1 – Absent

    2 – Adversarial

    3 – Fearful

    4 – Casual

    5 – Solemn

    6 – Intimate

3. How would you summarize your family's level of participation in spiritual activities?

    1 – Nonexistent

    2 – Rare

3 – Occasional

4 – Regimental

5 – Active

6 – Enthusiastic

4. How were spiritual discussions applied in your home?

1 – They weren't.

2 – To control

3 – To manipulate

4 – To teach

5 – To influence

6 – To reinforce

5. What was the perspective in your home in regard to moral absolutes?

1 – If it feels good, do it!

2 – There are no absolutes.

3 – Let your heart guide you.

4 – Dogmatic legalism

5 – Moderate conservatism

6 – Clear life boundaries

RESULTS

Above 24 = Strong spiritual legacy

19–24 = Healthy legacy

14–18 = Mixed legacy—good and bad elements

10–13 = Weak spiritual legacy

Below 10 = Damaged spiritual legacy

Note: If you are anything like us, the result of a quiz or test may leave you feeling something less than complete. However, the point here is to encourage you that no matter what your score, the legacy you determine to leave your children will most certainly be better than what you received, and for that, we can all be hopeful. Even if you scored high, there is always room for improvement. Remember:

> Whether you eat or drink, or whatever you do, do all to
> the glory of God. (1 Cor. 10:31)

CHAPTER SIX

YOUR EMOTIONAL LEGACY

MEET MIKI

Miki grew up in Japan. Every Sunday, she and her family went to church, and she had no idea why. It just seemed to be what people did. At church, her father was quite involved. People would tell Miki how blessed she was to have such a "wonderful, helpful father." But when Miki returned home, she would go to her room and cry. Confused and hurt, she often wondered who this man was that everyone else saw but she couldn't see.

Miki's father was seemingly a Dr. Jekyll at church as he played the part of a dutiful servant. At home, however, he transformed into Mr. Hyde, where he would physically abuse her mother and sometimes her.

"What are you wearing?" he once asked her mother. He didn't like her choice of clothing, so he grabbed her and threw her to the floor, tearing off her clothes.

When things like this happened, Miki would run and hide, trying to escape her father's wrath. She could never quite understand the opinions of others who called him "wonderful and helpful."

The family moved to the United States when Miki was in the third grade. It was the land of opportunity and hope, but it certainly did nothing to change the hypocrisy of her father. He continued to abuse Miki and her mom, until during one particularly bad fight, a neighbor came knocking on the door.

"This is America," the neighbor told Miki's father. "If I hear that you laid a hand on either of them again, I'll call the police."

Frightened by the threat, her father stopped the physical abuse. But his emotional abuse escalated.

When Miki was older, she grew proud of herself as she completed her two-year AA degree. She thought her father would be so pleased and impressed with her and that she would finally win his approval. Wearing her cap and gown and preparing to walk the stage to receive her diploma, she just *knew* her father would be there for her.

"Look what I did!" she said.

But he didn't even bother to look her in the eyes.

"Tell me when you graduate from a real college," were his only words.

Miki felt so hurt and rejected by her father once again that the emotional turmoil caused by his abuse over the years eventually led her to become suicidal.

BETTER TO GIVE THAN TO RECEIVE

Today, ministers and family counselors routinely treat the lasting effects of painful childhood memories such as Miki's. People from all walks of life struggle to overcome a negative emotional legacy that hinders their ability to cope with the inevitable challenges of life. Sadly, a solid emotional legacy seems to have become the exception rather than the norm these days. But it doesn't have to be that way. Whether or not you *received* a strong emotional legacy, you can still *give* one.

For those who have spent their entire lives trying to escape the past, it is difficult to comprehend the strength and stability that a positive emotional legacy can have upon future generations. To Miki, for instance, the celebration of Father's Day brought only pain.

Why would anyone want to dedicate a day to celebrate someone like her dad?

If thoughts of your childhood bring fear rather than fondness, imagine what it would be like for family memories to warm your heart rather than tighten your stomach. Now imagine yourself giving such feelings to your children. You can, and the first step is to understand what an emotional legacy should be and can be.

A strong emotional legacy will provide a child with healthy and balanced emotions that will allow him or her to be able to deal with the difficulties of life in a positive way. Here's a definition of a strong emotional legacy:

> A **strong emotional legacy** is an enduring sense of
> security and stability that is nurtured in an environ-
> ment of safety and love.

Let's break this definition down.

First, an emotional legacy is *nurtured* by parents. Nurturing takes time. The idea is to encourage somebody or something to flourish with much care. Therefore, you cannot build a solid emotional legacy quickly. Much like building a home out of brick on a solid foundation so that it can withstand the storms of life, it takes a lot of time and consistency to give your child a sense of emotional wholeness.

It might help us if we compared the emotional legacy to the planting of a tree. Some trees, as saplings, need a support to hold their small trunks against the wind. Most will need time to deepen their roots so that when a drought comes, they will be able to locate water down below. Without support and time, the tree is vulnerable to natural catastrophe—wind, drought, or pests. But once time has passed, the tree becomes strong and stable for many years to come.

The key to a tree's strength is deep, strong roots. In order to grow strong, the roots of the tree must be planted in rich soil and given adequate water and sunshine. So it is with our emotional legacy. We must create and maintain an environment that surrounds a child's fragile spirit with the nourishment required for healthy growth. This gives the child security and emotional stability.

Second, an emotional legacy *endures*. It is not quickly forgotten and will last throughout his or her adult years. When the child reaches maturity, the end of his or her childhood experiences becomes the beginning of an emotional legacy that continues throughout life.

Too often a parent's influence upon a child's emotional health is an obstacle to be overcome rather than a blessing to be cherished. Miki, for example, spent years dating abusive men who were disturbingly similar to her father, unable to recognize what a healthy male relationship actually looked like.

Not all adults had such a poor experience growing up. For instance, Miki's eventual husband, Brett, had a solid emotional legacy and today has had good success creating a strong emotional environment in their home. As a result, Brett has been able to help Miki learn to trust and grow. These two demonstrate how childhood experiences leave a dramatic imprint, even years after leaving home.

Third, a healthy emotional legacy *gives security and stability* when cultivated in an environment of love and safety. More than any other aspect of a heritage, the environment and tone of family life directly influence the outcome of our emotional selves. An atmosphere of love nourishes our emotional stability, thus giving us the capacity to cope with failure and pain. A sense of safety provides fertile soil so that we might feel secure and grow deep, giving us the confidence to face a harsh and often cruel world. If either love or safety is missing from the environment, deep roots are unlikely to develop.

As descendants of Adam and Eve, we are often plagued with doubt, fear, and insecurities. All of these things are native to what the Bible calls our "old nature." Emotional trauma makes us even more vulnerable to such harmful tendencies. Even authentic faith in Jesus Christ and the new life He offers do not magically remove the shrapnel of our fallen world and damaged emotions. But a strong, secure heritage can protect the fragile development of a child's emotional well-being by enveloping him or her in an environment of support. Hopefully, by this point, you can see the great importance of being strong in faith, as it goes hand in hand with feeling secure about who you are in Christ.

THE STABILIZER BAR

As an amateur stock car racer, Van Noble loved the thrill and challenge of simultaneously *going fast* while *staying safe*. Most fans love the loud engines, the screeching tires, the speed, and the possibility of a couple of dramatic crashes in every race. But they might also wonder how a driver can throw his car into a high-speed curve at nearly one hundred miles per hour. It doesn't seem rational. So what is it that keeps the car from crashing and burning at times like that? The stabilizer bar.

Affixed on the front end of the sophisticated suspension of the race car is a vital part called the stabilizer bar. Of course, it's not the only thing that creates stability, but it is extremely important. It keeps the car from swaying excessively while in a turn. It keeps both sets of wheels firmly on the track as the car negotiates the curves.

The emotional element of the heritage cord is like a stabilizer bar for the spiritual and social components. Many relationships have been lost because of unstable emotions producing irrational thinking and actions. Spiritual lives crash and burn every day while trying to navigate harsh circumstances thrown at them. Why? Because when children grow up in unstable families, their emotions become impaired. Without emotional health to give stability, the other two elements are pushed to the breaking point. As a result, relationships or spiritual lives or even both will feel the impact.

In Miki's case, she was raised in the church. In fact, her family attended quite faithfully. Unfortunately, the emotional legacy her father heaped upon her undermined the truth she may have otherwise learned. By the time she turned seventeen, she was convinced that there was no God. How could there be? Desperate for some kind of emotional relief, she prepared her bottle of pills, ready to end it all. She locked herself in her room and planned out her death, envisioning how it would affect her sister, her mother, and most of all her father.

Miki's stabilizer bar was broken, causing her to veer wildly from the spiritual heritage she had received. She also spent her days keeping quietly to herself, speaking little to others, and further isolating herself from those who might offer her some semblance of stability.

Her social and spiritual legacies suffered because of a damaged emotional heritage.

EMOTIONAL BARRIERS

There are many causes of emotional trauma, including abuse, mistreatment, and injustice. Many respond by giving up, withdrawing, or refusing to trust anyone. Some have been wounded so many times that they've learned to effectively "shut down" by defending themselves with harsh words, defensive actions, isolation, and a coolness toward anyone who might come around—friend or foe. They create an *emotional barrier*—shutting out anyone who tries to get close.

Meet Ginger. Ginger is the seven-year-old daughter of two Christian parents who are heavily involved with their church. Brad, her father, is a forty-year-old man who is a civilian worker for the air force. His wife, Anne, is a professional secretary. They are loving parents to their two children.

Ginger, however, started displaying signs that something was wrong—spitting at fellow classmates and her teacher and at times becoming almost uncontrollable with rage. Her mother was at a loss as to the reason for her violent outbursts. Ginger also began to gain weight quickly. Alarmed, her mother took her to the doctor, but he found nothing physically wrong. Initially, Anne essentially denied Ginger's problem, thinking that whatever was going on would eventually pass. But when Ginger's behavior persisted and she was almost expelled from school, Anne knew her daughter needed outside help.

At first, Anne turned to her pastor, who recommended professional counseling. She delayed the appointment for a time, fearing what she might discover, but eventually she gave in. As Anne described her daughter's situation in detail, it became clear that while Ginger was definitely a strong-willed child, her behavior was not consistent with a typical strong-willed temperament. It quickly became obvious that Ginger was creating an emotional barrier. Through her violent behavior, she had pushed away every friend or adult. Discipline didn't work, and as strange as it sounds, it seemed as if she was asking for some form of punishment for a burden of guilt she was carrying. When Anne attempted to pray with Ginger, she refused. She loathed church and would not participate in anything of a spiritual nature. All of her symptoms pointed to sexual molestation as the cause.

Hearing this, Anne and Brad both wept.

Ginger's immature emotions had been severely damaged. Perverted family members sometimes lurk in unsuspecting places, and in Ginger's case, the abuser was eventually discovered to be a trusted relative. Anne and Brad had done their best to guard against such a possibility, but had unwittingly failed.

Ginger's emotional barrier provided the only place for comfort. But as a result of her suppressed emotions, her relationships suffered, and her spiritual life was dying at the young age of seven. Ginger was completely off balance and in need of stabilized emotions. Each strand of the heritage cord had been thinned to become brittle and close to the breaking point.

While Ginger's situation was extreme, her response was all too common. It is normal for us, when violated, to build a barrier of protection, insulating us from further trauma. Spend time with any group of children, and you can pick out almost immediately the ones who are wearing some kind of protection for their emotions.

They hide from those around them until they determine whom they can trust.

Suppressed emotions are like an inflated beach ball being pushed under the water. It's not possible to keep a ball below the surface for very long! It will escape from under your control and resurface in another area of the pool, no matter how much pressure you exert on it from the top. Emotional problems, too, slip from under your control and show up elsewhere.

REPAIRING THE DAMAGED STABILIZER BAR

For Ginger, her suppressed emotional trauma was rearing its ugly head through both spiritual and relational conflict. Fortunately, Brad and Anne got help in tracing their daughter's symptoms to their root cause. Soon afterward, they began working to repair her damaged stabilizer bar. How? By giving her a safe, loving environment in which to deal with her pain. They helped her with a simple action plan.

1. RECOGNIZE AND DIVERT THE PAIN

Because Ginger's emotions were so severely damaged, it became necessary to *recognize* and *divert* the impact of her emotional pain. Notice that I did not say divert her *attention* from the pain, but divert *the pain itself* onto the stronger elements of her heritage cord—that is, the spiritual and relational. This can occur when Mom and Dad inject a strong sense of acceptance and demonstrative love.

Ginger's mom, dad, and brother created an environment of understanding and safety so that Ginger could recuperate from the trauma her fragile emotions had endured. The family watched for "warning signs" and reacted in love. Whether she was tired, angry, lonely, or confused, they responded with a healthy dose of relational support, which included prayer and reminders of God's love. They made every effort during those early days of healing to protect her from any unnecessary emotional stress. In short, they created a temporary detour so that God could begin repairing the damage.

2. DEMONSTRATE AND REINFORCE WHAT IS TRUE

Only God can truly repair the damage of emotional trauma; yet we can lend a hand by consistently *demonstrating* and *reinforcing* what is true. Whether he or she is dealing with divorce, alcoholism, physical abuse (as it was for Miki), or as in Ginger's case, sexual abuse, a child hurt by emotional trauma will be bombarded by lies that undermine the ability to see truth clearly. Lies such as the following:

> "You deserved it because you're a bad girl."
> "You can't trust anybody, not even Mom or Dad."
> "The molestation [divorce, rejection by a friend, etc.] was your fault."
> "This pain will never end."
> "God hates you."

During such accusing times, we must stand eye to eye with the truth. After all, God does not heal with deceit; He heals only with truth. To pretend the incident never happened or to sugarcoat the problem is not the solution. Sadly, that is exactly how most families deal with an emotional hit.

Fortunately for Ginger, she was allowed to face the truth, and healing has begun. The truths she recognized are truths that should exist in every family. Truths such as the following:

- You are totally and unconditionally accepted.
- Most people can be trusted … especially Mom and Dad.
- Healing will come in time.
- The trauma was not your fault.
- No one deserves what you went through. God does not punish us with such trauma.
- God does care, and He hates what happened to you.
- God doesn't hate you but rather loves you unconditionally.

As Ginger and her parents have discovered, when the truth is spoken, lies are broken. And when lies are broken, the emotional stabilizer bar can be repaired.

This same process is vital regardless of the specific source of pain. The need to repair the damage caused by divorce, the death of a loved one, betrayal by a close friend, peer rejection, or any other such "hit" is part of what a healthy emotional legacy will provide. Remember, even if your child has never suffered a major emotional trauma, providing the child with unconditional acceptance, consistent trustworthy actions, and a proper image of a caring God can give her or him a stable emotional legacy. It can also sustain a child if and when emotional trauma might occur.

3. GIVE YOUR CHILD A PLACE OF REST, NOT RESCUE

Perhaps the most difficult aspect of helping our children repair their stabilizer bar is avoiding the desire to rescue them. Everything within us wants to protect our children from all possible pain. But as Ginger's parents discovered, that is impossible. It is also harmful.

There are some things that our children must struggle through in order to mature. Our responsibility is to give them a safe place to learn and a loving environment in which emotional maturity can grow. We must somehow find the balance between providing a safe, nurturing environment in which they can rest from life's struggles and building a wall of protection that allows our children to escape from them. The former nurtures growth. The latter can create emotional cripples.

One day a man took a long walk and spotted a cocoon attached to a tree branch. He looked closely and thought a violent confrontation was taking place inside the caterpillar's temporary home. The cocoon was twitching vigorously. The man wondered if an intruder or a predator was stealing the cocoon for lunch. He moved in closer to peer through the translucent covering. He saw a tightly packed butterfly struggling wildly to free itself.

The man watched the poor floundering creature for a few minutes before he couldn't stand it any longer. He reached out and ripped open the remaining area of the cocoon, wanting to relieve the butterfly of its writhing struggle.

His intentions were good, but his assistance forever crippled the butterfly. What that man did not know was that the struggle strengthens the emerging butterfly's wings. As the fragile creature works through the difficult process of breaking free, it exercises its furled wings, pumping blood into the two appendages. The butterfly prepares for flight through this furious and wearying process. Sadly, the man's well-intentioned efforts served to doom the very life he had hoped to save.

We must not rescue our children from every difficulty; part of growing up demands that they learn to deal with difficulty themselves. But we can and should provide a refuge of support and safety through which that process can occur.

EVALUATING YOUR OWN EMOTIONAL LEGACY

To find out if you were given a strong or a weak emotional legacy, take a few minutes to complete the Emotional Legacy Evaluation as you did with the Spiritual Legacy Evaluation in the previous chapter.

As you answer the following questions, note that a strong emotional legacy is even more rare than a solid spiritual legacy for several reasons.

First, there is no user's manual for parents on how to create an environment that fosters the positive characteristics we've identified.

Second, emotions are tricky things, and the way one responds to the circumstances of life varies from person to person. For instance, two siblings who grew up in the same family might score their legacy on opposite ends of the spectrum, depending upon their personal experiences and the dynamics involved.

Finally, we are all prone toward failure. Intentionally or not, most parents tend to err to one extreme or the other, producing a less-than-balanced home environment.

The key is not whether your emotional legacy was perfect, but rather whether you've defined what characteristics you would like to build into the legacy you will pass on to your family. Even if you miss the mark in some ways, setting the right target is an important first step.

LEADING INDICATORS FOR AN EMOTIONAL LEGACY

Clearly, a strong emotional legacy offers a stabilizing influence for our children. We conclude our look at what constitutes a strong legacy by examining the leading indicators for an emotional legacy. What should we strive for, and what should we avoid in the process of creating an environment of love and security?

A STRONG EMOTIONAL LEGACY ...

- Provides a safe environment in which deep emotional roots can grow.
- Fosters confidence through stability.
- Conveys a tone of trusting support.
- Nurtures a strong sense of positive identity.
- Offers a "resting place" for the soul by creating a calm, loving atmosphere.
- Demonstrates unconditional love.

A WEAK EMOTIONAL LEGACY ...

- Breeds insecurity and shallow emotional development.
- Fosters fearfulness through instability.
- Conveys a tone of mistrust, criticism, or apathy.
- Undermines a healthy sense of personal worth.
- Causes inward turmoil.
- Communicates that a person doesn't measure up.

Don't be discouraged if you had more weak than strong characteristics in your legacy. Don't point an accusing finger at your parents. The past is the past, and it cannot be changed. It can, however, show us how to create a strong emotional legacy for our own children.

Miki grew up afraid of her father, damaged by his physical and emotional abuse. And after God worked in her life, Miki decided she would give her own two children something better. With the aid of her husband, Brett, she chose to become a source of spiritual strength and emotional encouragement to their children. In fact, they even adopted three more children. Now, every morning starts with a family hug—just one of many habits and traditions that help them give a better emotional legacy than they received. Miki can never change her past, but she has decidedly changed the emotional legacy she will leave her own children.

EMOTIONAL LEGACY EVALUATION

Answer each question by circling the number that best reflects the legacy you have received from your parents; then add together to find your total score.

1. When you walked into your house, what was your feeling?
    1 – Dread
    2 – Tension
    3 – Chaos
    4 – Stability
    5 – Calm
    6 – Warmth

2. Which word best describes the tone of your home?
    1 – Hateful
    2 – Angry
    3 – Sad
    4 – Serious
    5 – Relaxed
    6 – Fun

3. What was the message of your family life?
    1 – You are worthless.
    2 – You are a burden.
    3 – You are okay.
    4 – You are respected.

5 – You are important.

6 – You are the greatest.

4. Which word best describes the "fragrance" of your home life?

1 – Repulsive

2 – Rotten

3 – Unpleasant

4 – Sterile

5 – Fresh

6 – Sweet

5. Which was most frequent in your home?

1 – An intense fight

2 – The silent treatment

3 – Detached apathy

4 – A strong disagreement

5 – A kind word

6 – An affectionate hug

RESULTS

Above 24 = Strong emotional legacy

19–24 = Healthy legacy

14–18 = Mixed legacy—good and bad elements

10–13 = Weak emotional legacy

Below 10 = Damaged emotional legacy

CHAPTER SEVEN

YOUR SOCIAL LEGACY

Perhaps the most difficult strand of the legacy cord to grasp is the social one. Our social nature is complex—a mixture of *what we do* and *who we are*. Many variables exist within family relationships, and even more come from outside the family dynamic.

Here is our definition of the social legacy:

> A **social legacy** is giving a child the insights and skills necessary to cultivate healthy, stable relationships.

As they mature, children learn to relate first to family members, followed by relating to friends, peers, teachers, and eventually the "real world" made up of coworkers, bosses, customers, the butcher, the baker, and the candlestick maker. Relating well to others is vital to a successful life. And for better or worse, the primary classroom of relational competence is the home. That's why it is critical that we understand the importance of passing a solid relational legacy on to our children.

Consider Joel. He was the youngest of a relatively large Christian family. For the most part, his home was pretty healthy. But Joel struggled with relating to his peers. By the time he was ten, he was more comfortable hanging out with adults than with his classmates. By high school, his circle of friends had become small and selective.

Why? Joel had been raised to be *set apart* as a Christian. He was told to be careful about associating with the wrong crowd and to keep his faith strong. But despite his parents' best intentions, too much fun, in *his* mind, would lead to the *wrong* kind of fun. Joel's parents were correct in teaching him that he was set apart and therefore different. They were right to teach him to be careful about what type of friends

he chose and what he chose to do with his spare time. But Joel took it
to the extreme. He certainly didn't mean to, but he ended up becoming prideful, self-righteous, and unable to relate to others.

His parents were unaware of the problem. They were proud of
Joel and his accomplishments, but without them realizing it, Joel had
become friendless and isolated apart from only a few individuals. His
parents found out only when one day Joel came home from college
rather despondent.

"No one likes me," he confessed to his mother.

All of his efforts to "set a good Christian example" had made him
a rather unpleasant person.

What had Joel's parents missed? And what could they have done
differently?

Joel's parents missed the very important truth that a Christian
life has been designed to reach the people of the world. It's true—we
have been set apart, and we have already been declared righteous by
the finished work of Jesus Christ. But we are not called to withdraw
from this world or from those in it. Otherwise, how would anyone
ever see an authentic, Christ-centered life lived out? As Christian
parents, we need to take on our parenting with intentionality,
remembering that we are raising not only future mothers and fathers,
but also those who will make up the next generation of Christians.
As followers of Jesus Christ, we have been called to reach the world.
Second Timothy 4:5 states that we are to "do the work of an evan-
gelist" as part of our ministry. If we teach our children to stay only
within the confines of a "Christian bubble," how can we ever equip
them to live out this verse? Our children must learn to relate to all
different types of people.

If you want to see your children run a successful business, don't just train them in finance or management. Teach them about people. If you want them to become great teachers, don't simply educate them in the three Rs. Teach them about people. If you want them to rise above the odds, don't just make them tough. Teach them about people. The most significant skill you can give your child is not academic prowess or business savvy. It is the fine art of relating to people. Joel never learned to relate to a specific group of people: non-Christians. Why? Because his parents, in an effort to protect him, had raised him in an environment where non-Christians were rarely around!

Dale Carnegie, the guru of relational competence, put it like this:

> Dealing with people is probably the biggest problem you face, especially if you are in business. Yes, and that is also true if you are a housewife, architect or engineer. Research done a few years ago under the auspices of the Carnegie Foundation for the Advancement of Teaching uncovered a most important and significant fact—a fact later confirmed by additional studies made at the Carnegie Institute of Technology. These investigations revealed that even in such technical lines as engineering, about 15 percent of one's financial success is due to one's technical knowledge and about 85 percent is due to skill in human engineering—to personality and the ability to lead people.[1]

If that's true for people in the secular world and how they relate to one another, then how much more should we as Christians relate, not only to one another, but also to the lost world for which Jesus died.

Those who learn to relate well to others have an edge in the game of life. Those who don't are doomed to mediocrity at best and failure at worst.

Clearly, a strong social legacy is a great gift to our children, and the strength of this legacy depends, as do the spiritual and emotional components, on the parents' model. Consider your own home. If you grew up in a family that avoided conflict at all costs, you may have become a doormat. If your parents tended to shout or manipulate, you may struggle with shouting and manipulating as well. Patterns observed in childhood tend to show up in future relationships.

Of course, as adults we can change the pattern. We have the capacity and responsibility to grow beyond the foundation we were given. But it is much easier to cultivate healthy relationships today if we saw them modeled for us yesterday. That is why it is important that we give our children a better example than we might have received.

BUILDING BLOCKS

Many of us never saw healthy relationships in our own homes while growing up, making it difficult to model such relationships for our own children. So, what are some of the foundational building blocks for a solid social legacy? Although many could be cited, four stand out as essential. Model these for your children, and you will be on your way to building a solid social legacy.

1. RESPECT

As we saw in chapter 4, Billy had a weak spiritual legacy, which contributed to his anger and foul speech. But his appetite for stealing, fighting, and abusing his wife came directly from his lack of a solid social legacy. Unfortunately, neither his father nor his mother had any desire to build a relationship with Billy. They didn't respect him, they didn't respect each other, and they didn't even respect themselves. As a result, Billy inherited disrespect for others—including his own wife. He still loved her even though he didn't know how to show her.

To properly understand what it means to respect someone, we must first understand the root of our respect. Respect is inseparably linked to value. We respect that which we value. If we value a person, then we are saying that we see the person's worth, purpose, and importance, and thus we show him or her our respect.

If you remember my (Jack's) heritage story in chapter 2, my mother's pregnancy with me was, in my father's eyes, unwanted. The child—me—was an interruption to his life, and so my father displayed his impatience with me through his yelling and/or silence. It was not a healthy relationship. I now believe this all came from the fact that he did not place value on my life. Thus, he had little or no respect for me. In all fairness and in honor to him, toward the end of his life, he shared with me that he saw what God had done in my life and with the church, and that he was proud of me. Those statements carried great weight for me, even as a grown man, because they absolved the past. More importantly though, I got to hear my *earthly* father giving praise and honor to my heavenly Father, much as it says in Matthew 5:16 (NASB):

Let your light shine before men in such a way that they
may see your good works, and glorify your Father who
is in heaven.

Respect, then, begins within each individual and works its way
out to others. If you do not respect yourself, then how could you
respect anyone else? If you do not respect your own possessions, then
most likely you will not respect the possessions of others. This is one
reason God told Adam to "keep and dress" the garden. We develop
a healthy respect for the things we put effort into. Adam could sit
back after a hard day of work in the garden and appreciate his efforts.
That time of reflection creates a deepening desire to build up and not
tear down.

Billy admits he never learned that principle. In his own words,
"What I possessed I got without ever trying. I never needed to sit at
the end of a day and reflect on what I had accomplished. In fact, I
mocked and laughed at those I had duped and ripped off."

It is obvious that Billy was never taught about the love of God.
From an early age, a child needs to understand that he or she is
greatly valued by God. The estimation of ourselves is not what gives
us value; rather, we receive value through God's love for us (John
3:16).

A good practice for any parent is to begin nurturing within his
or her child a respectful spirit early on. This can simply be taught
by instructing them not to break things or throw things and telling
them to be nice to their dolls or toy trucks. Respect for property,
then, will ward off vandalism and stealing. Respect for people will
ward off violence and immorality.

In Joel's case, he considered non-Christians somehow less worthy of respect. Respect, in his mind, was only for those who deserved it. He didn't understand the difference between *earned* respect and *entitled* respect.

Earned respect is what we give to those who, in our opinion, have done something worthwhile. It is subjective and exclusionary. It is also easy. After all, it is easier to give respect to those we admire or consider successful.

Entitled respect is different. It is given regardless of one's perceived worthiness. We show proper respect to the president of the United States, for example, even if we disagree with his politics. Why? Because he is entitled to that respect due to the office he holds. Likewise, every human being is entitled to respect because he or she occupies the "office" of one made in God's image.

The first building block of a strong social legacy is insisting that members of the family give and receive the respect to which they are entitled, whether they have *earned* it or not.

2. RESPONSIBILITY

Everyone makes mistakes. But blaming others for those mistakes, rather than taking personal ownership or responsibility, creates distrust and bitterness. When I do all that I can to *earn* the respect of others, rather than simply relying on *entitled respect*, then I am taking responsibility for my actions. In many ways, respect leads to responsibility, the second factor in creating a strong social legacy. Self-respect, then, means that despite the circumstances you have been raised in, despite the situation you find yourself in, you will not look to justify your failures through blaming others, but will instead take responsibility for what you can control *today.*

Jim, the friend we mentioned in an earlier chapter, felt he had every reason to blame others and walk down a path of self-destruction. His dad left the family to follow after sensual pleasures when Jim was still very young. His mother reacted by turning inward, becoming consumed with her own loneliness and suffering, forcing her son to practically raise himself. By all accounts, Jim had every right to continue a negative, self-centered pattern. After all, he had been cheated out of a strong heritage, right? He could have given up, made wrong choices, and thrown responsibility and respect to the wind. But he didn't. Instead, he took responsibility for his own attitudes and actions. As a result, today Jim models a picture of responsible manhood for his wife, young son, and others. The cycle has been broken because Jim refused to play the blame game and accepted his responsibility as a husband and father.

Demonstrating responsibility to your children starts while they are still young. It means, for example, showing them a contrite heart when you make mistakes and asking them for forgiveness when necessary. It means following through on a promise made even if it now seems pointless or too difficult.

We can impart responsibility to our children as well by assigning duties at home. Giving children specific responsibilities can infuse a sense of self-respect, as does giving them room to make their own mistakes. After all, it is when we are allowed to make mistakes or to fail that we are taught wisdom, values, and the stewardship of responsibility.

3. LOVE AND ACCEPTANCE

I love my children unconditionally—I can't imagine anything they might do that could make me stop loving them. Yet, when they were growing up, there were times when my children behaved in ways that were not acceptable. Whether they talked back or communicated more profound disrespect, our children surely faced consequences for their sin. As the Bible states in Galatians 6:7:

> Do not be deceived, God is not mocked; for whatever a
> man sows, that he will also reap.

As parents, we need to let our children suffer the consequences of inappropriate behavior. Letting our children face consequences can teach them both respect *and* responsibility. Yet we often fail to distinguish our *unconditional love* of that person from the *conditional acceptance* of his or her behavior. When that happens, we risk our children believing that they are accepted and loved only if they perform to a certain level or expectation. To counteract such parental infractions, we need to verbalize and demonstrate love to our children with no strings attached. This love—the kind that says, "I love you no matter what"—contributes to strong, healthy relationships with family members, friends, and coworkers. As a result, our children can feel free to make and learn from their mistakes without the fear that we will stop loving them.

What exactly, then, is the difference between unconditional love of the person and conditional acceptance of behavior? Well, God demonstrates *unconditional love* by providing salvation for all:

But God demonstrates His own love toward us, in that
while we were still sinners, Christ died for us. (Rom.
5:8)

Yet, God also demonstrates *conditional acceptance* by disciplin-
ing sinful behavior:

For whom the LORD loves He chastens,
And scourges every son whom He receives. (Heb. 12:6)

Similarly, in our relationships with our children (and in every
healthy relationship) we must balance *unconditional love* with
conditional acceptance of behavior. We should expect our children
to obey because it is the right thing to do; and because we love
them, we desire them to understand the great blessing that comes
from obedience. Therefore, when they disobey, we shouldn't protect them from the natural consequences or the fallout of their
sin. It is unwise to think that we can always prevent those we love
from making foolish or sinful choices. We must let them suffer the
consequences of their behavior, which also allows them to learn
from and ultimately take responsibility for their actions. After all,
protecting those we love from the consequences of foolish living
prevents maturity and ensures continued folly. If they accidentally
burn themselves, they will probably realize the danger of playing
with matches.

In the meantime, tell your children you love them. Part of giving
a solid relational legacy includes making sure our kids know that
they are totally, unconditionally loved—even when they fail. But at

the same time, we must be certain they realize that some behaviors will not be accepted. And we can do this by establishing and enforcing rules in the context of a loving, supportive relationship.

4. BOUNDARIES

Setting boundaries is not just helpful for building strong relationships—it is essential for the social welfare of our children. A Minnesota Crime Commission report offered this assessment of children and delinquency:

> Every baby starts life as a little savage. He is completely selfish and self-centered. He wants what he wants when he wants it: his bottle, his mother's attention, his playmate's toy, his uncle's watch. Deny these and he seethes with rage and aggressiveness, which would be murderous were he not so helpless. This means that ALL children, not just certain children, are born delinquent. If permitted to continue in the self-centered world of infancy, given free rein to his impulsive actions, every child would grow up a criminal, a thief, a killer, a rapist.[2]

We as parents have but maybe a short eighteen years to civilize our children and prepare them to be released into society as productive citizens. That assignment includes establishing boundaries that frame how children should relate to God, authority figures, their peers, their environment, and their siblings.

Many years ago when our children were quite young, we took a trip to see the Grand Canyon in Arizona. We could hardly wait to get to the edge of the canyon. It just so happened that we came to an area where there was no railing, and our six-year-old daughter, in her excitement, ran right to the edge. She kept leaning over a little more and a little more. When we finally saw her, she had gone way beyond where she should've been. We quickly grabbed her back and scolded her for getting so close to the dangerous edge. She looked puzzled at our reaction, for she saw no boundary markings that would've given her an awareness of where she could stand and look into that gigantic hole. She was completely unaware of the danger before her.

As this story illustrates, children need to know where the markings and boundaries of obedience are. Our children will never understand those boundaries unless we communicate our expectations. Unless we convey the protective purpose of boundaries our children will never see the need to obey. God Himself doesn't ask us to walk in obedience without first communicating to us what He desires of us.

Here are some of the questions our children will need to answer on their journey to adulthood. These are excellent questions for parents to ask their children as well as themselves as they establish proper boundaries in the home:

- How far can I go in challenging authority before I've crossed the line into disrespect?
- How should I respond when I am treated unfairly?
- How important is my tone of voice when I talk to my parents and others?

- When, if ever, is losing my temper appropriate?
- Where do my rights end and the rights of others begin?
- Is it ever okay to fight?
- How should I react when others are treated wrongly?

The list could go on and on. Such questions should be answered at home to help establish and aid children in understanding healthy boundaries. Doing so gives children a protective side rail, allowing them to enjoy the journey rather than fear every dangerous curve.

RULES WITHIN RELATIONSHIP

A word of caution: boundaries are typically expressed as rules, so they work best when given with a healthy dose of love.

Jason, for example, learned right from wrong while growing up. But the moment he became old enough to make his own decisions, he rejected most of the values Mom and Dad had taught. Why? Because rules were given in a relational vacuum. Jason's parents gave the right medicine, but it wasn't served with the spoonful of sugar—namely, a strong, loving relationship. They loved Jason but were also distant, having a hard time demonstrating that love. Honest, open communication rarely occurred, so Jason had no forum to discuss, ask about, question, or challenge his parents' "list of rules." And so, rules without relationship often fuels rebellion.

Adam and Eve were given rules, or rather a single rule: do not eat from a certain tree in the garden. But they weren't left to simply obey a cold mandate. Rules were given in the context of relationship with the rule-giver Himself, almighty God. God explained to Adam how much freedom there was under His rule:

> And the LORD God commanded the man, saying, "Of every tree of the garden you may freely eat; but of the tree of the knowledge of good and evil you shall not eat, for in the day that you eat of it you shall surely die." (Gen. 2:16–17)

Notice that He gave the consequence for disobedience. "This is what is best for you," God was saying to Adam. "I've given you everything else because I love you. Please, I beg of you, do not eat that which will end in death." (Of course, we all know how that story ended.)

Similarly, God gave the Israelites the law of Moses. In it, they were warned about disobedience. But they were not just left to obey some cold, unreachable rules. Just as God walked and talked with Adam in the cool of the day, so He dwelled with Israel in a pillar of cloud and fire and spoke through Moses. What God wanted from both Adam and the Jewish nation was a relationship. He knew how important it was to their well-being.

God desires a relationship with our children. He didn't just open the back door of heaven and holler out some vague instructions as to how we are to live this life and prepare for eternity. He sent His Son to show us. He knows our pain and is acquainted with our weaknesses. He sent His Holy Spirit to dwell in us, to bear witness that the relationship will continue forevermore.

If parents force-feed rules without a personal relationship, they are setting their children up for rebellion. But giving the same set of rules within the context of a healthy relationship will foster respect and responsibility.

EVALUATING YOUR OWN SOCIAL LEGACY

Let's take a look at the social legacy you were given in order to evaluate the relative strength of this element of your cord. Complete the Social Legacy Evaluation, remembering that, like the evaluations in the two previous chapters, this exercise is designed to help focus your attention on both the good and the bad elements of your heritage. No one received a perfect heritage. In fact, if you score well on even one or two of the three, you beat the odds. Sadly, a strong heritage is the exception, not the norm.

Here's a final reminder as you consider your legacy evaluation scores in chapters 5, 6, and 7. If one or two of the scores are very weak, don't give up on your ability to pass along a new, stronger heritage in place of the one you received. Some feel that if part of their heritage is weak, they must reject the whole thing.

Sarah was given a wonderful spiritual heritage, yet she rejected it. Why? Because her relational legacy was weak, driving her to rebellion. Unable to distinguish one strand of the cord from another, she rejected all of it. Bad move on her part!

Frank, on the other hand, was given a terrific relational and emotional legacy but chose to leave both behind. Why? Because his parents failed to give him a spiritual foundation. So when he became a Christian as a young adult, he began viewing everything his parents did as substandard. That's unfortunate, because his parents did a great job on two aspects of the heritage they left him. Frank should have kept the good and built on it, rather than rejecting it all.

While it is dangerous to overly divide the spiritual, emotional, and relational aspects of our heritage, it can also be helpful. It allows us to identify and replace the bad while keeping and building upon the good.

THE LEADING INDICATORS FOR A SOCIAL LEGACY

Once again, a strong social legacy provides the foundation for cultivating healthy, stable relationships. We've touched upon several aspects of this process already. Let's briefly list some of the leading indicators we should be instilling in our own children before evaluating the social legacy we've inherited.

A STRONG SOCIAL LEGACY ...

- Sets clear boundaries on how to treat others appropriately.
- Teaches respect for all people.
- Instills a sense of responsibility for the feelings and property of others.
- Balances unconditional love for the person with conditional acceptance of behavior.
- Enforces rules in the context of a loving relationship.
- Models clear and sensitive communication skills.

A WEAK SOCIAL LEGACY ...

- Causes confusion regarding what is appropriate treatment and what is not.
- Treats others with disrespect.
- Follows a "survival of the fittest" perspective.
- Accepts wrong behavior in the name of love.
- Is dictatorial, enforcing rules.
- Models poor interpersonal communication.

Which of the two extremes is closer to reality for you at this time? More importantly, which represents what you want to give from this day forward?

SOCIAL LEGACY EVALUATION

Answer each question by circling the number that best reflects the legacy you have received from your parents; then add together to find your total score.

1. Which words most closely resemble the social tone of your family?

1 – Cruel and abusive

2 – Cutting sarcasm

3 – Chaotic and distant

4 – Noncommunicative but stable

5 – Secure with open communication

6 – Loving and fun

2. What was the message of your home life in regard to relationships?

1 – "Step on others to get your way."

2 – "Hurt them if they hurt you."

3 – "Demand your rights."

4 – "Mind your own business."

5 – "Treat others with respect."

6 – "Put others before yourself."

3. How were rules set and enforced in your home?

1 – Independent of relationship

2 – In reaction to parental stress

3 – Dictatorially

4 – Inconsistently

5 – Out of concern for my well-being

6 – In the context of a loving relationship

4. Which word best characterizes the tone of communication in your home?

1 – Shouting

2 – Manipulative

3 – Confusing

4 – Clear

5 – Constructive

6 – Courteous

5. How did your family deal with wrong behavior?

1 – Subtle reinforcement

2 – Accepted in the name of love

3 – Guilt trip

4 – Severe punishment

5 – Discussion

6 – Loving, firm discipline

RESULTS

Above 24 = Strong social legacy

19–24 = Healthy legacy

14–18 = Mixed legacy—good and bad elements

10–13 = Weak social legacy

Below 10 = Damaged social legacy

CHAPTER EIGHT

GIVING BETTER THAN YOU RECEIVED

In chapter 8 of the book of John, we are told of a situation regarding a woman who was caught in the act of adultery. The Pharisees brought her to Jesus, as they hoped to trick Him into violating one of the laws of Moses. They knew that Jesus was a man of compassion and forgiveness and that He would probably just say to forgive her and let her go.

It's interesting to note that the text states that these men somehow caught this woman in the very act. How did they do that? Did they know about her sin already? Was one of the "accusers" also her lover? And if so, why was the man not taken as well? After all, a woman can't be caught "in the very act" all by herself.

CONDEMNATION

The Pharisees came with the woman in tow and began asking Jesus what should be done to her. They knew that the law said quite clearly that she should be stoned to death, but they asked Him nonetheless.

Jesus then stooped down and began to write with His finger in the sand as though He wasn't listening to them. They continued to press Him until He stood in their presence and made a profound statement: "He who is without sin among you, let him throw a stone at her first" (John 8:7).

Then He stooped down and began writing again. The people were probably quite curious as to what He was writing. Some have suggested that He was writing down the sins of the accusing men, from the oldest to the youngest, for they began walking away as each felt the prick of conviction in his conscience.

Compassion

Then Jesus and the woman were left alone. Jesus stood and, seeing no one but the woman, asked her, "Woman, where are those accusers of yours? Has no one condemned you?" (John 8:10).

She replied, "No one, Lord."

Jesus said to her, "Neither do I condemn you; go and sin no more" (v. 11).

It would be good for us to know that when Jesus released this woman from her sinful situation, He was in fact saying to her that she had been given a new life and didn't need to live the life she had once known. Regardless of whether this had been a possible setup by the religious sin-sniffers and faultfinders, the woman was still the one who had put herself into a compromising situation. But why, and what was it about her that led these people to target her for such an entrapment?

Remembering yet Changing

I would never pretend to read more into this situation than what was intended. But it seems that something in this woman's past had convinced her that she had less value than others. Perhaps she was prone to seeking out approval or acceptance through the attention of a man. Maybe she grew up without the love of her father. Had she come from an abusive home? We don't know the details of her past. What we do know is that God Himself overruled her past. From that moment on, she would view her past in light of her new beginning. Whatever damaged heritage she had been given was now buried in the love and forgiveness of God incarnate. This would be something that she would have to remember for the rest of her life in order to stay on the right track.

We can all relate to the struggle of past memories attempting to revisit us in our thoughts and dreams. But we are encouraged in Scripture to bring those thoughts under the captivity of Christ (2 Cor. 10:5), which means that we are able to counter the assault and go on the offensive whenever those ugly thoughts resurrect themselves.

Starting Over

To know that God has forgiven us is a wonderful truth. But understand this: God also has the power to forget about our past, a truth I have found absolutely liberating! God can do this because of His divinity. For those who have come to trust in His unfailing word, Isaiah 43:25 promises, "I, even I, am He who blots out your transgressions for My own sake; and I will not remember your sins."

For us, unfortunately, forgetting is not so easy. You and I are tempted to nurse and coddle our hurt feelings and memories. We need to understand that Jesus not only forgave this woman and set her free, but also will do exactly the same thing for each of us. This releases us from the grip of those hurtful memories, bringing us into a new life. That's the power behind giving a stronger spiritual legacy than you received.

Your Turnaround

In the previous three chapters we learned about the three strands in the heritage cord, and you evaluated your personal heritage. A healthy spiritual strand gives us the discernment to make decisions about right and wrong according to the Word of God. A healthy emotional strand serves as a stabilizer, connecting and balancing the spiritual and social strands. A healthy social strand allows us to grow into responsible citizens, placing relationships ahead of our own selfish desires. We saw how each strand may have been weakened as we grew up and where we might need help with our own families.

But *understanding* the weaknesses in our heritage cord is only part of the solution. Homes are riddled with folks who *understand* they aren't doing things right but are at a loss as to how to make the necessary adjustments to give something better than they received. It's time to combine the three legacy evaluations and form a course of action that can break the generational cycle—a course of action that can change tattered rags into beautiful robes. And just as there are three strands to the heritage cord, we recommend three steps toward making your personalized plan: look back, look up, and look ahead!

Step One: Look Back

If you haven't already, complete the evaluations found at the conclusion of chapters 5 through 7. Then, take a hard and honest look at those evaluations. Review your scores, and then complete the following Personal Heritage Survey.

PERSONAL HERITAGE SURVEY

This exercise is designed to help you discover the relative strength of the heritage you were given. As you answer the following questions, try to identify the good to keep, the bad to discard, and the weak to strengthen. Drawing from the earlier evaluations, circle the word that best describes the heritage you received.

MY SPIRITUAL HERITAGE WAS:

Strong   Healthy   Mixed   Weak   Damaged

MY EMOTIONAL HERITAGE WAS:

Strong   Healthy   Mixed   Weak   Damaged

MY SOCIAL HERITAGE WAS:

Strong   Healthy   Mixed   Weak   Damaged

In the following sections, check the boxes that indicate whether what you received was strong or weak in the following categories.

YOUR SPIRITUAL STRAND

Did any of these apply to your upbringing? Mark all descriptive statements that match what you received.

A STRONG SPIRITUAL LEGACY ...

- ☐ Acknowledges and reinforces spiritual realities.
- ☐ Views God as a personal, caring Being who is to be both loved and respected.
- ☐ Makes spiritual activities a priority in life (church attendance, prayer, Scripture reading, serving, etc.).
- ☐ Talks about spiritual issues as a means of reinforcing spiritual commitments.
- ☐ Clarifies timeless truth and right from wrong.
- ☐ Incorporates spiritual principles into everyday living.

A WEAK SPIRITUAL LEGACY ...

- ☐ Undermines or ignores spiritual realities.
- ☐ Represents God as an impersonal being.
- ☐ Never or rarely participates in spiritual activities.
- ☐ Has few spiritual discussions of a constructive nature.
- ☐ Confuses absolutes and upholds relativism.
- ☐ Separates the spiritual from the practical.

YOUR EMOTIONAL STRAND

Did any of these apply to your upbringing? Mark all descriptive statements that match what you received.

A STRONG EMOTIONAL LEGACY ...

- ☐ Provides a safe environment in which deep emotional roots can grow.
- ☐ Fosters confidence through stability.
- ☐ Conveys a tone of trusting support.
- ☐ Nurtures a strong sense of positive identity.
- ☐ Offers a "resting place" for the soul by creating a calm, loving atmosphere.
- ☐ Demonstrates unconditional love.

A WEAK EMOTIONAL LEGACY ...

- ☐ Breeds insecurity and shallow emotional development.
- ☐ Fosters fearfulness through instability.
- ☐ Conveys a tone of mistrust, criticism, or apathy.
- ☐ Undermines a healthy sense of personal worth.
- ☐ Causes inward turmoil.
- ☐ Communicates that a person doesn't measure up.

YOUR SOCIAL STRAND

Did any of these apply to your upbringing? Mark all descriptive statements that match what you received.

A Strong Social Legacy ...

☐ Sets clear boundaries on how to treat others appropriately.

☐ Teaches respect for all people.

☐ Instills a sense of responsibility for the feelings and property of others.

☐ Balances unconditional love for the person with conditional acceptance of behavior.

☐ Enforces rules in the context of a loving relationship.

☐ Models clear and sensitive communication skills.

A Weak Social Legacy ...

☐ Causes confusion regarding what is appropriate treatment and what is not.

☐ Treats others with disrespect.

☐ Follows a "survival of the fittest" perspective.

☐ Accepts wrong behavior in the name of love.

☐ Is dictatorial, enforcing rules.

☐ Models poor interpersonal communication.

Finally, record any additional thoughts that might describe the heritage you were given. Take a few moments to contemplate these questions. Also, you may wish to include your spouse. Sometimes painfully honest insight from our better half is exactly what we need to face the truth about how our pasts have bled into our present relationships.

- What things did you appreciate about your home life?
- What things caused the most pain?
- What things have you taken for granted over the years?
- What negative issues may be impacting your attitudes and behaviors today?

Now that you have spent some time looking back, you are ready to move on to step two: look up!

STEP TWO: LOOK UP

The process of honest evaluation will lead many to the realization—some for the first time—that they have unresolved issues to confront: someone to forgive, a painful emotion to release, fears to overcome, or bitterness to confess. You may recognize troubling truths that you should acknowledge or a personal weakness you need to admit. Whatever the issues, deal with them once and for all. Don't allow their cruel grip to keep you in bondage to your past. You can be free. Look up. Seek the Lord for what you need. From God you can find:

- The grace to forgive and be forgiven.
- The strength to admit your weakness and accept help where needed.
- The faith to accept what is true, even when your emotions betray reality.
- The confidence to give the Lord the reins of your life, especially during those times when you feel out of control.

Talk with the Lord about whatever is on your heritage list. Ask Him to help you deal with whatever you find there. Believe me, He is more than able to do so! Remember that a conversation goes two ways. If all you do is tell God your troubles but don't listen for what He has to say in return, you aren't really looking up to Him—instead you are looking inward.

God gave us three very practical ways that allow us not only to *talk* to Him but also to *listen* to His instruction.

First, He gave us the holy Scripture. We live in such a blessed time in the United States where access to the Bible is often taken for granted. It wasn't always like this. In other times and places, people have been willing to die for the right to read and protect God's Word. Today, few of us have even read through the entire book that we supposedly base our faith upon. The Bible isn't just a collection of stories and lineages. It reveals who God is and what He is like and gives us clear instructions on how we are to live our lives. Believe it or not, that also includes our role as parents!

Second, He gave us the Word incarnate: Jesus Christ, our Lord and Savior. Jesus came not only as both God and man but also as the sacrifice for our sin. He was a living, breathing example of how we should live our lives.

Third, He gave us our spouses. This is not insignificant. Marriage is a great mystery, one that Paul called a symbol of the union between Christ and His bride, the church. There is no greater spiritual institution given to us than that of marriage. Contrary to what we have been brought up to believe, marriage is actually not about you or me. It is about you and me being like Jesus to our spouses. Marriage is a ministry, and from it others should see a better picture of what

God is like and how He relates to His church. Aside from God, no one knows a man more intimately than his wife, and no woman should be more transparent with anyone else than she is with her own husband. Husbands and wives should be able to lean on each other and encourage each other.

You must look up to God for the answers: by telling Him your hurts, admitting your failures, then listening to His counsel through His Word. Only then can you look ahead.

STEP THREE: LOOK AHEAD

Once you have identified the reality of your past and invited the Lord to help you confront any unresolved issues, changes can begin. The following exercise, "Designing Your Heritage," will help you to envision the heritage that you are seeking.

As you complete the exercise, remember that the purpose is to identify a specific goal. The old adage is true: those who aim for nothing are sure to hit it. But with the outcome from this exercise you will have a target you can really shoot for. Completing this exercise is an important step on the road to giving a positive heritage.

Designing Your Heritage

This exercise is designed to help you identify the heritage you want to impart to your family. Drawing from your responses in the Personal Heritage Survey on page 139, list the "strong" characteristics from each category (spiritual, emotional, and social) that you would like to be able to pass down. Don't allow doubt or insecurity to hold you back. In the blanks below, list what you want it to be. Ephesians 3:20 says, "Now to Him who is able to do exceedingly abundantly above all that we ask or think, according to the power that works in us." God wants you to expect more than what you can imagine for your life. Set the bar based on God's standard, not so that you will fail but so that you will continually stretch yourself beyond what you believe yourself capable of!

Using the spaces provided, list the characteristics that you intend to give. Circle the letter *K* for "keep," because they were solid aspects of the heritage you were given. Next to those that you consider weak in your own heritage, circle the letter *S* for "strengthen." Finally, next to those items in your heritage that you want to *change* in some way in order to improve upon them, circle the letter *C*. This step will become important later as you build your heritage plan because it will help you zero in on those areas requiring the most intentional effort.

The spiritual legacy I want to give: Category

_____ K   S   C

_____ K   S   C

_____ K   S   C

The emotional legacy I want to give: Category

_____ K   S   C

_____ K   S   C

_____ K   S   C

The social legacy I want to give: Category

_____ K   S   C

_____ K   S   C

_____ K   S   C

In the chapter that follows, we will present our Turnaround Toolboxes. These are practical ways that can help strengthen the legacy you leave. Use these ideas as presented, or as inspiration for other ways to take the action plan you created in this chapter beyond an ideal to reality.

CHAPTER NINE

TURNAROUND
TOOLBOXES

In earlier chapters we've described the multigenerational impact of the spiritual, emotional, and social legacies. We've also guided you through the process of assessing the strong and weak elements of the heritage that you received in your home while growing up. Hopefully, you have also begun to form a vision for the kind of heritage you hope to give to the generation after you.

Now comes the fun part: practical ideas for starting the turn-around. As we enter into this section of the book, it's important to loosen up a bit and make this fun. We all love humor, and God has made us to appreciate humorous moments in life, so let's put on our seat belts and step out into some adventures that will no doubt challenge us to break out of our comfort zones.

TOOLBOX #1

FOSTERING MARITAL INTIMACY

The best gift you can give your children is to foster a strong, healthy marriage. By nature, children watch their parents. The message we send by the way we talk to and touch our spouses not only acts as a powerful witness but also sets the atmosphere of our homes. A warm and loving home fosters the character traits of the fruit of the Spirit: love, joy, peace, long-suffering, kindness, goodness, faithfulness, gentleness, and self-control (Gal. 5:22–23). This list of fruits not only is beautiful but also creates a fun, happy, and healthy environment. Children need to see their parents—either weekly or, at the least, monthly—protect as sacred the all-important date night. If you aren't already in the habit of dating your spouse, then borrow from the following ideas as a starting point. Use them as a springboard to come up with your own list. Be creative, and think of ways to have fun together like you did when you first met! And insist on one important rule of engagement: *no cell phone/texting allowed except in life-and-death emergencies!*

Déjà Vu: Go back to the location where you first met or had your first date, if possible. (If not, reenact your encounter by going to a similar location.) If you went to a restaurant, try to recall what you ordered. If you saw a movie together, go rent it and watch it again (if appropriate). Try dressing up in the same style of clothes that you remember wearing. Talk about and try to re-create the conversation and the emotions that you were feeling. You'll both laugh and discover how each of you viewed that first encounter.

Dine "Out" at Home: Create a special environment for your children in one of their rooms with games, books, and pizza. Then have a special dinner prepared for just you and your spouse. Depending on the time of year, you can light a fire in the fireplace or sit outdoors. Make sure to set up an intimate table with candles, flowers, etc., and enjoy each other's company. Your family will probably get a kick out of seeing you together in a romantic setting. Don't be surprised if you catch a couple of "lookie-loos"!

Drive "In" Movie: If you are on a tight budget and can't seem to find any privacy and/or a babysitter, then create your own drive-in theater right at home. Pop a healthy supply of popcorn for you and your family. Either put your children to bed, or give them a movie of their own to watch and their own bowl of popcorn. Then take a short walk to the driveway with your spouse, and put your favorite movie in the DVD player in your car or on your laptop. If you don't own a laptop computer, see if you can borrow one for the night. You'll have privacy, spending little or no money all while making a fun memory!

Romantic Sunset Gazing: Pick the best location in your area to watch the sunrise or sunset. After consulting a timetable for either of these daily occurrences, make your way there with a basket of either coffee and doughnuts or a thermos of soup and bread. Settle into your front-row seat and watch the big event. Take time together to praise and thank the Lord for His amazing artwork!

Mystery Train Trip: Go to the nearest train station with a picnic. Depending on your sense of adventure and the train schedule, decide on the spur of the moment where you would like to go. Keep in mind that your next stop could be either a mile or ten miles away. You could choose to picnic on board or at your destination—or just simply eat at a café once you arrive wherever you are going. You may want to exchange or make up stories along the way about your travel journey. (If there is no train station nearby, you could do the same thing on a bus or even a taxi.)

Becoming Kids Again: Make an afternoon of all the things you loved to do as children or always dreamed about doing. Did you love to ride the carousel? Is there one nearby in town? Were you a finger-painting artist? Paint away! Maybe just the simple things of life were

most exciting, like swinging on swings at a park or eating ice cream.
Be sure to allow yourself to be silly and have fun!

Flights of Fancy: Drive to the closest international airport. Park in
the short-term parking lot, and take a stroll through the international terminal. The range of nationalities found there is stimulating.
Go to the airport café and "people watch" while making up your
own stories as to where different people are going and why they are
traveling. Then take a look at the flight schedule, and decide where
you would go at that moment if you could. Then, as you drive home,
be thankful that you won't be sitting on an airplane for the next
eleven hours!

Scenic Walk/Ride: Determine a location in your area that lends itself
to a beautiful walk or bike ride. This doesn't cost a thing, and yet
the time spent together outside is immeasurable. Enjoy lighthearted
conversation all along the way—and the fresh air will do you good!
If possible, stop for a snack or bring along your own.

Anniversary Notes: It shouldn't have to be said that an anniversary,
a birthday, and Mother's Day or Father's Day are a must to keep
special! Don't forget to let your spouse know how very important he
or she is to you. Put up a chalkboard or bulletin board in a public
space so all can see that you both make each other a priority. Leave
love notes, verses, and inspiration to build confidence in each other,
not only on those special days but also throughout the year. And
know that your children will be encouraged and blessed to see this
display of written affection as well!

Field Trip Date: For a very simple, cost-free date, try window-shopping. Take turns deciding where you will go. No matter what the other person chooses, wear a smile and watch, enjoying your spouse's enthusiasm toward whatever his or her interest is. For instance, Lisa loves going to antique stores. I, at first, went along just to be a good guy. After a few trips, I realized that I had become interested in all the items that brought back nostalgic memories of my childhood. Come on, guys, when was the last time you saw a Tonka truck made out of real metal?

Strong Marriage Annual Plan: This may seem frightening at first to think about, but the goal is to set a plan in action so that activities and dates will actually take place! In order for your marriage to stay fresh and exciting, you need to purposefully set time aside on your calendar just like you would for an appointment for anything else. It may seem as though the spontaneity of a "date" will be taken out, but the reverse will happen as you see it as a priority and something to look forward to. This "plan" may seem unimportant and unexciting, yet without it, you and I both know that consistent dates will never happen. If it's on the calendar, you are more inclined to keep the appointed date night and make it something that you actually look forward to. Make it sacred, make it holy, and make it happen! Bring your calendar or PDA on the date for scheduling purposes. Each spouse is to give dates and times that he or she is available each month and then prioritize these days. Use the following questionnaire to help set a plan into action. Select one of the ideas given, or create your own to put on your schedules.

Question: What can you do as a married couple to protect the time that you need to encourage healthy communication?

☐ Schedule an evening walk together twice a week

☐ Schedule a date night twice a month

☐ _____

_____

Question: Do any of the following issues need improvement in your marriage? If so, decide what action should be taken. For example, you might decide to read a book on the subject together, attend a class on a particular topic, or seek godly counsel or advice.

☐ Shared vision and goals

☐ Better communication

☐ Romantic intimacy

☐ Managing money

☐ Parenting the kids

Our plans include the following: _____

_____

_____

Question: When can you plan a weekend away together to recharge your batteries and rekindle romance? _____

_____

Where would you like to go that you could afford? _____

_____

Who could watch the kids? _____

_____

Question: How can you help each other improve physically and emotionally?

- ☐ Work out together
- ☐ Eat out less often and instead cook healthy meals at home
- ☐ Give each other time alone with God by watching kids, etc.
- ☐ _____

_____

Question: When will you incorporate the habit of praying together?

- ☐ At the end of our evening walks twice weekly
- ☐ Before going to sleep each night
- ☐ _____

_____

The Love Journal: A love journal is a great way to open up sharing with each other since it is often easier to express feelings and appreciation in writing than it is to do so face-to-face. Purchase a journal or notebook that is nice, a little above the schoolroom version, so as to keep it special. Designate a location where you will pass the journal back and forth, such as the bathroom sink counter or each other's pillows. You may want to mark your calendar on specific days or once a month when you want to be sure that you take the time to write a love note to your spouse. Dedicate the first page of your journal by writing words of love, encouragement, and blessings. *This is not a place to write negative or critical comments.* Make sure to note the date of when you write your love notes so that you can look back and see the special things you have written to each other over the years. You might also include some of the fun things you have done together. Use the following as ideas to help craft meaningful love notes:

- *I Appreciate You:* Share the gratitude you feel for how your spouse serves and sacrifices for the family.
- *I Admire You:* Let your spouse know the qualities that you see in him or her such as character, persistence, patience, grace, strength, etc.
- *I Affirm You:* Tell your spouse when he or she responds well to different situations or circumstances.
- *My Prayer for You:* Write out a prayer for your spouse. This can be a great opportunity if you know about something specific happening that day that he or she might be worried about.
- *Just Because:* You can simply write, "I want you to know how much I love you and am so thankful to be married to you!" or you can write out three pages explaining your feelings. It's up to you—it's not important how long the note is, but how heartfelt it is.
- *Special Occasions:* Take some time for a birthday, anniversary, or holiday to share a love note in your journal. Be specific about the occasion, and write in a context that will be meaningful to your spouse.

TOOLBOX #2

FOR PARENTS OF YOUNGER CHILDREN

Raising children in this day and age can be challenging. Sadly, many young families have fallen into a trap that has engulfed their everyday lives with technology, entertainment, and organized sports programs. While all of these things have their proper place and are of value, none should ever supersede the importance of family time together and establishing God as the priority for how family members interact with one another.

The following toolbox is designed to help you focus—and for some of you, *refocus*—on the importance and the power of spending both quantity and quality time with the younger ones. Here are several ideas that support giving a strong spiritual, emotional, and social legacy to children who are between the ages of toddlerhood and elementary.

<u>Modeling God's Character:</u> When our children are very small (birth to about three years old), we make an imprint on their lives more by how we treat them than by instructional activities. It is in this season that we impress things on their hearts, not their heads. Because children form their early view of God largely from how they view their parents, we can use the early years to reinforce the character of God—including both His love and His justice.

- **God's Love:** The best way to impress the love of God .upon the hearts of our children is by doing what comes naturally. We should overwhelm them with affirmation and affection—including lots of hugs and kisses and praise for their fledging attempts to talk, walk, and feed themselves. In these small ways, we are demonstrating unconditional love and the kind of affection God has for us. (By the way, don't stop as the child ages!)

- **God's Justice:** In addition to establishing the security of unconditional love and affection, it is important to establish a clear sense that Mom and Dad set the rules and that the child is expected to obey those rules. Starting at about eighteen months, establish some consistent system of discipline when your child willfully defies your rules. We demonstrate God's character when we refuse to tolerate rebellion against the rules we've established. Please note, however, that there is a difference between willful defiance and childish irresponsibility. Like God, we must clarify right from wrong with children and bring about appropriate discipline when those rules are violated. Parents who neglect this principle during the early years risk giving children the mistaken idea that love and justice are mutually exclusive. God is both, and we must model both. Some excellent resources to help you implement this balance include *Dare to Discipline* and *Hide or Seek*, both written by Dr. James Dobson.

Thankful Guessing Game: This game can make car trips more enjoyable for young children and shows them that God is the provider of everything. It can also help develop within them a heart of thankfulness and praise. You can start by taking turns describing something for which you are thankful, such as, "I am thankful for something that keeps me warm and has a zipper and two pockets." The children would answer, "Your sweatshirt!" Next, you could say, "I am thankful for something that keeps me warm in the winter and cool in the summer. It takes me all around and wherever I need to go." They would answer, "The car!" You get the idea, I'm sure. You can come up with tons of things to make the game exciting and fun and to generate hearts that are full of gratitude. Examples: the Bible, food, clothing, toothbrush, water, police, firefighters, nurses, doctors, etc.

Baking Lessons: Baking cookies, cupcakes, etc., can provide a great lesson about the importance of following instructions. Let children know that a proven, trustworthy recipe, if followed, will result in a yummy treat. The activity can also show the importance of patience and learning how to wait while all the ingredients are baking in the oven. To teach this lesson, you will be baking your own trusted recipe by yourself while allowing your children to use the same ingredients—but without exact measurements and/or instructions. Let them make it as they desire. You can let them measure as they wish, stir, and put it all in their baking pan. (Yes, it will be a little messy.) Bake the items simultaneously in the oven, knowing that your recipe will be the yummy treat and theirs will not. Lesson learned: after the baking is finished and you sit down to try both masterpieces, your children will see a great difference in the two finished products. Take this opportunity to share with them about the importance of following directions, and let them know that disobedience leaves only a bad taste! As Proverbs 4:13 says, "Take hold of my instruction; don't let them go. Guard them, for they are the key to life" (NLT). Good things will come out of your children's lives when they follow God's clear instructions in the Bible. His recipe for life can be trusted.

Lessons in the Garden: You can teach valuable lessons when you step outside and look around at God's creation. Purchase inexpensive seeds, and plant them either in the ground or in a pot. Share with your child how God supplies the power and information within the seed to sprout and grow. Take time to explain how unattractive the seed is but that it will eventually produce either a beautiful flower or a yummy vegetable or fruit. The seed looks dead and yet will bring forth new life. It's a great example of resurrection, too! Let your children have a part in planting, watering, and caring for their new little plant. It will be quite exciting to them as they see its growth. An additional lesson is showing them a place where weeds have overtaken an area. Explain that a garden needs constant care or else the weeds will choke out all the good plants. This is what sin does in our lives when we don't maintain good habits for our growth, such as reading our Bibles, praying, serving others, etc. You could even teach the parable of the sower, using seeds and acting it out (Matt. 13:1–23). Use a children's Bible to make the story more understandable.

Good Samaritan: On the first day of school, read the story of the Good Samaritan (Luke 10:25–37) in an easy-to-read version. Tell your children to look for ways to imitate the kindness of the man in the story. Instruct them to always be searching for ways they can help other people, regardless of the children's age. Either once a week or once a month, at dinnertime or bedtime, have them share the different ways in which they were able to be a Good Samaritan.

Have a Heart: We know a family that started a thoughtful tradition within their home that teaches their children to be looking for the good in others. The mother sewed a little red heart with a pocket on the side of it, and when she spotted someone in her family doing something kind or favorable, she wrote a little note and put it inside the pocket. Then she left it on the person's pillow or somewhere else he or she could easily find it. The recipient would then be on the lookout for someone else doing the same type of kind act or something he or she could thank that person for. The next person would then write a note of encouragement or thanks and pass it on *secretly*. No one could know who the heart came from, but everyone was to keep passing it along throughout the family. When doing this activity, tell your children not to keep the heart for longer than a week, as it will lose its appeal if it is not kept moving. This activity teaches the children to always be looking for good in others instead of focusing on the bad.

Reclaim the Lost Art of Reading: In this day and age dominated by passive technologies, it's easy to let your computer or iPad take the place of one-on-one moments with your child. Don't discount the great significance of reading books. Take every opportunity while your child is young to instill within him or her a love for good literature. There are so many books that can shape a child's view of right and wrong and instill a desire for moral character. Let your children pick out their favorites to read in the afternoon or at bedtime. Every so often, take a trip to the library or a Christian bookstore, and let them pick out a new book. You can even find good used books inexpensively at a thrift store or on the Internet. When our daughter was around two or three, we made an audio recording of our bedtime reading to her, and her responses are priceless to this day!

Building Unity: Give each person in the family at least one item from the recipe that you are making. If they are old enough, let them measure it accordingly. Have them taste their ingredient, and see if they think it tastes good all by itself. It will most likely be undesirable, but when mixed with all the other ingredients and cooked and/or baked, it will be delicious. Let them know that living alone and isolated does not contribute to family life, but working together as a team does! As Psalm 133:1 says, "How wonderful and pleasant it is when brothers live together in harmony!" (NLT).

Don't Forget to Be Silly: Invest in good Christian children's music such as Mary Rice Hopkins, Psalty the Singing Songbook, and others. There are great lessons and qualities to be learned through some of these catchy songs. Don't be afraid to dance and be silly with your children so that they can see that knowing God and doing His will can be a lot of fun. Lisa and I would like to add that even though these CDs might seem dated, they are still as good for young children today as they were for our children back in the 1980s! In fact, our grandchildren are now listening as well.

Mad Hatter Tea Party: How about a tea party where everyone dresses up and wears the craziest hat he or she can find? You could help them make their own or just grab one from your closet and add embellishments to it. You could try this on a rainy day when it's too wet to play outside. And anything can go with tea (or chocolate milk if the children are too young for hot tea). You could serve little cakes or just good old peanut butter and jelly. Or better yet, make it a high tea, where all of you put on your finest dress-up clothes, use your best manners, and eat scones with lemon curd (a great way to introduce a little culture to their young lives). Either way it's sure to please!

Family Nights: When your oldest child turns about four or five, begin a weekly or semiweekly routine called Family Night. Start out with some crazy dancing to a fun theme song and then lead a short, object-lesson-based activity that creates wonderful family memories while teaching your children something about God and biblical values. Here is one simple example:

> Five-year-old Kyle and three-year-old Shaun stare at Dad seriously contemplating his rather deep question. "How could God be real if we can't see Him?"
>
> The oldest takes the lead. "That's a good question, Dad!"
>
> "Well, is there anything else we know is real but we can't see?" asks Dad.
>
> "How about air?" suggests Mom.
>
> Dad then pulls out several balloons. They inflate them.

"Air is real enough to expand these balloons. I bet air has power, too," Dad says while releasing his balloon. Now Shaun, the three-year-old, is really engaged! After ten minutes of intense competition over who can make their balloons fly farthest, Dad introduces a little slogan for tonight's activity. "Just like air, God is there!"

A lasting impression was made. In fact, ask either boy (now young adults) about how God can be real even though we can't see Him, and they will immediately respond, "Just like air, God is there!" Ask them what that means, and they'll explain. "God is real and has power, even though we can't see Him."

You can start the family night routine in your home today. Take advantage of either of the following resources to learn how.

- The Family Night Tool Chest Series by Jim Weidmann and Kurt Bruner, available from heritagebuilders.com
- *Just Add Family: Easy Recipes for Faith-Filled Fun* by Kurt and Olivia Bruner, available from familylife.com

TOOLBOX #3

FOR PARENTS OF OLDER CHILDREN

The adolescent years can be tough on parent and child alike. But with a lot of love, attention, and strong family traditions, you can make the transition a little easier. Dr. James Dobson, in his wisdom, shared that the beginning years of puberty are a huge challenge for most young teens as their hormones fluctuate and cause havoc to their bodies and emotions. If you can offer a little extra patience and understanding during those first couple of years, the remaining teen years should be much less traumatic. But if we enter those years unprepared and fail to give our kids the grace and kindness they need, then the adolescent years can be disastrous. Here are several ideas for giving a strong spiritual, emotional, and social legacy to children in the adolescent years. Pick and choose the impression points that will work best for your family.

Portion Controls: One of the most challenging areas for parents with older kids in this day and age is media. Teens are bombarded with outside influences that distract them from real relationships and undermine the wholesome values and Christian beliefs you have tried to pour into their lives from birth. When it comes to television, Internet, mobile devices, and the like, families have more coming at them than ever before. Just like with food, we must establish "portion controls" for all media. It is okay to set limits on and say no to unhealthy access to certain technologies, even when your teens protest that "everyone else has it!" But be sure to model it yourself first. If we parents constantly text or surf the web, then why should our kids take our demands seriously? If we aren't eating healthy, then why should they? Older children watch whether we actually "walk the talk"—or whether we just give them a list of expectations we don't apply to ourselves.

The Look-Out Game: When out with your older children, be looking for ways in which to teach your teens to be on the lookout for others in need. You can turn it into a game by suggesting that as you are out doing errands, shopping, etc., they should say, "Look out!" when they see someone in need. You should then take the time out of your busy schedule to teach them a valuable lesson in giving and caring. Drive through a fast-food restaurant or go to some other place that you can purchase some inexpensive food, and buy it to give away. Have your child be the one to extend this act of kindness. You can also keep Christian tracts handy in your car to hand out to bless those in need of God's love. Another idea is to keep a well-supplied box of nonperishable goods in your trunk that you can readily hand out.

Camera Fun Day: Make a day of running errands, shopping, or just hanging out more fun by taking pictures throughout the day of the strangest places you can find to document on film. You could develop a theme, like "Saturday afternoon fire hydrants," where you snap shots of one another (or just your teen) atop every hydrant you come across that day. Nothing spiritual here … just having fun and making memories.

Chalked: When we were young, kids used to go out and toilet paper people's houses for fun. It's pretty much frowned upon in this day and age (and in some places, illegal), not to mention expensive. Instead of that, how about having your teens go "chalk" a friend's driveway? Since your teens probably can't drive (or even if they can), do this as a family. Agree upon whose house it is they would like to visit some late evening. Then dress in black (for fun), and with chalk in hand (bought at the dollar store) take turns tracing your kids' outlines, feet, hands, etc., on the friend's driveway. Finish off by writing, "You've been chalked!" and then add your favorite Bible verse or a comment that will bless the family.

Scavenger Hunt Cookies: Let each of your kids invite at least one friend over some evening. Have a scavenger hunt in your neighborhood for cookie ingredients. Let the children collect only one item per neighbor. When they return, bake the ingredients together as a group/family. When finished, take some of the cookies to the people who gave you ingredients, and bless them back!

Family Game Night: Don't forget the fun of some friendly competition with board games. If you don't already have some, you can make a small investment and create memories that last. It's a great way to teach your teens (and yourself) how to lose graciously and how to win respectfully. Our adult children still have their favorites, and we love to play whenever we can.

Giving Out: To train your teens to be looking for ways to be compassionate to others, when you drop them off at school, ask them to be looking for those who might need encouragement or just a good word. Teens can often be so self-centered that they rarely look at the needs of others. Give them a challenge of searching for ways to give out kind, truthful compliments or to express a word of encouragement for something they see others doing. It might even be a word to a teacher who is having a bad day. At dinner, ask them if they were able to accomplish this task. At first, it might be uncomfortable for them, but as you encourage *them* with a good word, they, too, will learn how to have the "eyes" of Jesus!

Be That Place: Make your home a place your child's friends want to be. Many of us know what it was like growing up in a home filled with stress, tension, or boredom. Lisa grew up in a home kids did *not* want to visit. Even she sneaked out on occasion! That's why when we became the parents of teens, we had an open-door policy. Friends were always welcome. We had a very small home, and it was always filled with smelly teenagers! But we knew what they were watching, what they were doing, and what they talked about. We had snacks, and we invested in a big trampoline and later even added a pool. We wanted them to feel right at home. Make your home a place your teens' friends want to be.

Movie Night Chats: Ask any teen his or her favorite activities, and I guarantee that watching movies will be at or near the top of the list. Why not "go with the flow" of a teen's interest by leveraging films to spark spiritual discussions? Just as kids are more likely to embrace our beliefs if they enjoy our company, teens are more likely to talk about something they already find interesting.

There is nothing complicated about watching films to discuss key themes and scenes. Most of us do that naturally. But here are a few practical tips to keep in mind.

- **Select Wisely:** Not every film is worth watching or touches on important themes. Select a film that can trigger meaningful dialogue. Ask people you trust what films they have seen that have been worthwhile. You may want to start with several of the films summarized with discussion questions at MovieNightChat.com.

- **Watch Intentionally:** It is easy to turn the passive activity of watching movies into an intentional opportunity for discussion. Before starting the film, make it clear to everyone involved that you want to talk about the film from a Christian perspective afterward. Ask each person to make a mental note of specific scenes that reinforce or undermine his or her beliefs while watching the movie.

- **Discuss Openly:** Take a few moments after watching the film to enjoy open dialogue about what you've seen. Invite one person to lead everyone through the process, and insist that no one person dominate the conversation—including Dad or Mom! Remember, the goal is not to teach or even to agree on everything. The goal is to foster healthy conversation and sharpen everyone's critical-thinking skills.

- **Make It Fun, Not Forced:** You want to avoid turning movie night into an agenda-driven duty. Keep it relaxed, and make the time together fun. For example, you might want to let one of the kids facilitate the discussion rather than doing it yourself. You'll also want to take turns selecting the films so that you hit everyone's interests. And resist the urge to interrupt the film. Let everyone enjoy the full story first, waiting until the end for discussion.

- **Discussion, Not Diversion:** Many of us watch movies as "mindless entertainment." That is fine from time to time. But when scheduling a movie chat, remember that the goal is meaningful discussion. Don't feel you need to limit yourself to films that affirm your faith. In fact, movies that oppose Christian beliefs can trigger great discussion, especially with mature teens.

- **Prescreen to Avoid Surprises:** Unfortunately, most popular films contain offensive content such as foul language, sexuality, or gratuitous violence. Parents should try to prescreen films to avoid surprises. Even if someone you trust recommended the film, it is wise to check it yourself since people often forget or underestimate the content of certain scenes. I recommend reading detailed descriptions of troubling content by title on websites such as PluggedIn.com. You might also consider investing in a tool that pre-edits offensive content, such as ClearPlay.com.

TOOLBOX #4

FOR GRANDPARENTS

Bill Cosby once said, "A grandchild is God's reward for raising a child." I would say that if God were to allow us an opportunity to be more like Him, then it would be called grandparenting. It's hard to think of a more powerful and influential calling within the family structure than that of a grandparent. God has designed a child to naturally gravitate toward his or her grandparent, and that opportunity should never be wasted.

Grandparents seem to have an air of divinity in their favor. They get to do things with their grandchildren that would otherwise be a big no-no, like eating ice cream just before bed or having peanut-butter pancakes with whipped cream (a favorite here in our home). But the best part of grandparenting isn't just the fun and games. It is the high and holy ministry that has been given to us. For example, we can show a greater and deeper level of grace more often than busy and pressured parents.

Being grandparents allows one of the most wonderful opportunities known to man—teaching children about life from our vantage point. We have a special place that allows us the freedom to communicate to them about who Jesus is, the power of prayer, the Bible and science, the importance of character, history near and far, and the need for patience and the love of God. Grandparents are generally not in the busy hustle and bustle of everyday life and therefore tend to have more time in their day to just listen and allow children to ask as many questions as they want. They have the time to "smell the roses" and take a walk, go to the park, or play a board game.

Be creative on your own, or use the ideas below to become more
intentional about giving your grandchildren a strong spiritual, emotional, and social legacy. Use them as a springboard to create lasting
memories all along the way.

Travel Back: Take a trip to a 1950s diner with your grandchildren.
Order some burgers and milkshakes, and then take the time to share
with them what it was like in the years when you were growing up
(whether that was the '60s, '70s, or even '80s) and what you loved
about being a kid. Talk about when you were young and what kinds
of things you did for entertainment before the age of cell phones,
computers, and electronic gadgets. You might even be able to find a
drive-in burger place or a drive-in theater.

A Memory Lane Adventure: If at all possible, drive to where you
grew up, and show them the house you used to live in. Tell them
about the things you liked to do, where you went to school, what you
did with your friends. Maybe even drive by the church you attended,
if applicable. Share the highlights of your childhood, and let your
grandchildren know that you are praying that these years for them
would be as unforgettable as they were to you.

Long-Distance Lunch: Use the Internet not only to talk with your
grandchildren but to see them as well. Use whatever way is accessible
on your particular computer to connect visually and audibly, and
then set a certain day and time each week to eat a meal with them.
Make it a special time; maybe it's Saturday lunch with Grandma and
Grandpa, no matter how many miles are between you. Don't forget

to pray with them before your meal and to let them know that you pray every day for them, whether they are at school or at home. You can start building a relationship right away with that child and not miss out on the simple everyday pleasures of life.

The Great Outdoors: The lessons are endless when you step outside of your home. Talk about our Creator God and how He is the One who has made absolutely everything that we see. Start a special garden with the children, and let them see the rewards of hard work, tender care, and maintenance. We, too, must maintain our relationships with God and our family and friends. If we don't, we will have an overgrown garden full of weeds, with no good fruits coming out of it.

One Hundred Percent Americana: Set up a lemonade stand in front of your house or near a local park. You can make unusual flavors like apple lemonade or pineapple lemonade along with the traditional favorite. Choose to either sell the lemonade or give it away. If you choose to sell it, take the money earned and give it to someone in need. It's a great way to show your grandchild the faithfulness of God, who freely provided the lemons so that we could freely bless someone who needs His love.

God Made the Clouds: We all love to stare at clouds, but it's even better when you are with your grandkids. You can watch as the clouds change from an elephant into a Mickey Mouse head and then into a dragon. Teach the children about how God is the One who made the clouds and how He blesses us with rain. Let them know that one day Jesus will return in those wonderful clouds. The importance of living their lives in a way that pleases and blesses Him is a good lesson to share with them. Share about heaven and how beautiful it is and that one day we all will be there together. Tell them what the Bible says about heaven and what it looks like. Great conversations start with the simple things of life.

Thankfulness: Take a tour of your local firehouse. Share with the grandkids how important it is to be thankful for those who risk their lives to keep us safe. Call ahead to make arrangements, and ask if the children can climb on the fire truck, sit inside it, and/or have a tour of the station. Your grandchildren will be impressed and a bit more patriotic the next time they see a fire truck and hear the siren. You could even have them help you bake some cookies to thank the firefighters for all that they do.

Short Picnic Trip: If money is an issue (or even if it's not), you can teach your grandchild to make the best of any situation. This is a great discipline to nurture. Things may be tough financially in some homes. So go on a picnic in your own backyard. Set out a blanket, and bring some music and a Frisbee. Some of the most meaningful things in life don't have to cost a thing!

Cultural Experience: Add a bit of culture to your grandchild's life by taking him or her to the symphony, a concert, a ballet, a play, a museum, etc. Parents don't often have the time or money to give their children such experiences. Why don't you? Use the occasion to enjoy one another's company, model social skills, and point out likely religious influences on the artist, writer, musician, or historical figure involved.

CHAPTER TEN

A WORD TO PASTORS

by Pastor Jack Hibbs

I seem to have an anticipation disorder, if there is such a thing. Rather than simply enjoying reading a book from start to finish or watching a movie through its entirety, I find myself instead trying to figure out how it will conclude. For example, when I first became a Christian and began reading my Bible, I didn't start in the beginning with Genesis but immediately turned to the back and started reading in the book of Revelation to find out how it would all end. I thought, *Why wait?* So while praying and toiling through this book, I have given much thought to its conclusion; not just how to wrap it all up, but also how the topics we've addressed would relate to the "end of the story."

In the past few years, we've seen an increase in the breakdown of the family. More and more of our counseling appointments have had to do with marriage problems, parenting issues, and especially blended family difficulties. I believe that this is not just a season or a cultural anomaly but rather the reaping of what has been sown into the structure of the family for well over fifty years. We are now harvesting the bitter crop of the women's liberation movement, the pursuit of materialism, the devaluing of human life, the attack on marriage, and the epidemic of absentee fathers. Unless these trends are reversed, our nation will continue on a downward slide that will destroy the institution of the family as we know it.

To those who think I've overstated the problem, I would ask, "What direction do you see the family heading in, and what are you willing to do to turn it around?" These are the questions that confront every leader in the local church today, myself included.

That's why our church launched a ministry specifically designed to help our families turn things around. In 2011, we began what we call @HOME. This is a ministry that was created to give people the tools and support necessary to foster intentionality when it comes to creating a God-honoring marriage and family life. As part of this exciting initiative, we created a physical and online resource center where people can freely take practical tools for every life season and family dynamic.

Our @HOME ministry exists to create God-honoring families one step at a time. We have two simple goals: (1) make family intentionality easy by providing useful tools and helpful ideas for making Christianity real at home, and (2) make family intentionality more likely by running periodic campaigns that emphasize specific habits such as praying together, discussing faith around the table during family meals, making marriage date nights a priority, and others. The entire strategy is designed to help parents and grandparents fulfill the commandment found in a familiar passage of Scripture:

> You shall love the LORD your God with all your heart, with all your soul, and with all your strength.
>
> And these words which I command you today shall be in your heart. You shall teach them diligently to your children, and shall talk of them when you sit in your house, when you walk by the way, when you lie down, and when you rise up. You shall bind them as a sign on your hand, and they shall be as frontlets between your eyes. You shall write them on the doorposts of your house and on your gates. (Deut. 6:5–9)

As a pastor, I can't tell you how satisfying it has been to know that we are equipping families for success and that the fruit of this investment will pay great dividends for generations to come.

I hope you will consider joining the growing movement of pastors who are making the home a priority. The model we have implemented is available for customization at your church. Visit DriveFaithHome.com to learn more.

LEADING AT HOME

Scripture teaches us that leading well at home is the proving ground for leading God's church. Consider the job qualifications detailed by the apostle Paul in letters written to two of his first-century cola-borers and overseers, Timothy and Titus. Paul listed several items every applicant's résumé had to include, such as being "blameless, the husband of one wife, temperate, sober-minded, of good behavior, hospitable, able to teach; not given to wine, not violent, not greedy for money, but gentle, not quarrelsome, not covetous; one who rules his own house well, having his children in submission with all rever-ence" (1 Tim. 3:2–4).

Why? Because in Paul's words, "If a man does not know how to rule his own house, how will he take care of the church of God?" (v. 5).

If family life breaks down, your wife and kids will most likely come to resent the ministry that you have worked so hard to build. Children naturally perceive God through the lens of what you do, not just what you say. When a minister's wife and/or kids feel neglected at home, they might begin to blame the ministry. They may become disillusioned or walk away from the faith that the minister proclaims to others. And our Enemy knows that. He has used failure at home to destroy far too many good pastors, leaders, and churches.

Warning signs include—but are not limited to—physical exhaustion, emotional depletion, lack of vision and inspiration, and spiritual dryness. The fact that you still pray over your meals and that the family attends church on Sunday does not necessarily mean you have a Christ-centered home. It takes husbands and wives nurturing joy in each other's lives rather than staring at each other with the droopy eyes of ministry fatigue and burnout.

It takes dads and moms investing in the faith of their children as an example to the rest of the congregation, rather than attending to the congregation at the expense of their own children.

The church fills a support role when it comes to the spiritual formation of children, but it is the parents who are called to do the heavy lifting. That is God's model, and it has worked for thousands of years where and when applied properly.

I consider serving the Lord as a pastor an amazing honor and privilege, to say the least. But that calling includes the responsibility to inspire and equip others to lead well at home. Every parent is the spiritual authority to his or her own children, and no one can point a child to Jesus Christ better than Dad or Mom. Church leader, parents need our encouragement not only to attend church on Sunday as Scripture teaches but also to live out their biblical faith at home every day and in every situation. And as leaders, we must show the way.

Deuteronomy 6 says that it's the parent's responsibility first and foremost to teach spiritual understanding to their children as they sit, walk, and lie down. That's full-time ministry, if you ask me!

Can I encourage you, colaborer? Let's inspire our flocks to live out their faith where it matters most—in the home. Only then will the next generation of believers see church as an exciting, necessary, and active part of the greater Christian experience. Unfortunately, many are missing out because they see Christianity as a Sunday-only thing.

THE FINISH

There is a lot of talk these days about revival. I've heard and read about so-called revivals happening in almost every religion, if you base it on numbers. For example, Buddhism is experiencing what some are calling a revival. Islam, in its push toward world dominance, has also been described in terms of revival. But when I as a Christian talk about revival, I'm not talking about what I've seen in recent years within the church as to its physical growth or even the megachurch movement. Don't get me wrong—I am not putting down church growth. According to whomever makes up these definitions, I happen to be a pastor of a megachurch, whether I like it or not. Keep in mind that the apostle Peter preached a sermon on the southern steps of the temple in Jerusalem, and some three thousand people became believers on that day! That's a megachurch. But if our churches and families are going to advance into this century on mission, on target for Jesus Christ, then we will have to do so by returning to the authority of the Word of God and by living in obedience to it.

I was extremely blessed to have come out of the Jesus People Movement of the 1970s. That move of God, which began in Southern California, not only dramatically countered the counterculture of humanism and hedonism (sex, drugs, and rock and roll), but also affected Christians, causing them to thirst again for the Word of

God. People sitting in dead or sleepy churches rose up from their Lazarus-like sleep and walked into churches that had begun teaching the Bible again—the whole Bible and nothing but the Bible. It was an awesome sight to see! I remember showing up to church over an hour early just to get a seat *on the floor*! When those hippies of the '60s and '70s got saved, they went out and began to tell everybody about Jesus and His power to change lives. They began living in such a way that Jesus became attractive to the lost around them before the lost ever had a chance to read a Bible. The witness of those believers produced a hunger within unbelievers. Hundreds bowed their knees to Christ each week and were baptized. The day that I was baptized, I was one among some five hundred others.

The movement in which I found Christ was later recognized as an official "revival" by Dr. J. Edwin Orr, a church historian expert on the subject. Not just because tens of thousands of hippies got saved and decided to leave their drug-induced craze to follow Jesus, although that was amazing in and of itself. But I am also convinced that revival started within God's people as they returned to the authority of Scripture and with a passion to genuinely worship Jesus Christ.

Here at Calvary Chapel Chino Hills we are seeing an increasing number of young people coming to Christ. Many of them tell me about their lifestyle, which includes sex, drugs, and the pain that an aberrant use of the Internet can cause. Some are only twenty to twenty-five years of age, yet in some ways, they're going on fifty. They desire genuine change in their lives that only Jesus, through the power of the Holy Spirit, can bring. They often have come because a Christian friend has influenced them and invited them to consider Jesus.

What would happen if our churches and homes were on the same page? Can you imagine if what we lived out in the church was the same life lived out in the home? What if it became normal for the church and the home to once again model Jesus as Lord in all the areas of life?

This book was written to help you ignite genuine faith in your own home and in the homes of those attending your church. If that happens, then we as a family, a church body, a community, and a nation will begin to see a complete turnaround for the good. I want to encourage you to take the time to read the appendix written by our coauthor, Kurt Bruner, to learn how your church can join this movement that will, we pray, make us a more worthy witness for Jesus Christ in these last days.

A MOVEMENT OF TURNAROUND CHURCHES

by Kurt Bruner

You've probably heard the statistics. For more than a decade, church leaders have been bombarded by one report after another suggesting that churched kids are rejecting Christian faith at an alarming rate. The data strongly suggest that less than half of those who grow up in church remain active believers as adults. And the problem is not with what's happening at church—but with what's not happening at home. That's why I have been honored to partner with leaders like Jack and Lisa Hibbs as they seek to turn the tide of generational faith decline. How? By creating a culture of intentional families. Consider the following reports on recent trends.

Declining Christian Affiliation: According to a 2001 study conducted by the Graduate Center of the City University of New York, large numbers of American adults are disaffiliating themselves from Christianity. US polling data from the study indicate that of those who identify themselves with a specific religion, only 76.5 percent identified themselves as Christian—a drop of nearly 10 percent in one decade.[1] This decline matches trends observed in Canada between 1981 and 2001. If the trend continues, Christianity will become a minority religion in the United States by the year 2042.

The End of Christian America: "The percentage of self-identified Christians has fallen 10 points in the past two decades," *Newsweek* reported in April 2009.[2] A recently released survey on American religious identification also revealed that the percentage of those who identify with no religion at all has doubled since 1990. These trends reinforce findings summarized in the 2007 book titled *unChristian: What a New Generation Really Thinks about Christianity* by David Kinnaman and Gabe Lyons. The authors found that the increasingly negative perception of the Christian faith has been fueled by the fact that most of those who consider themselves non-Christian in America are actually former church kids. As the book explains, "This leads to the sobering finding that the vast majority of outsiders in this country, particularly among young generations, are actually *de*-churched individuals."[3]

Losing Our Teens?: In October 2006 the *New York Times* ran a cover story with the headline "Evangelicals Fear the Loss of Their Teenagers." The writer reported that "despite their packed mega-churches … evangelical Christian leaders are warning one another that their teenagers are abandoning the faith in droves."[4] The paper publicized a movement that has been growing to reinvest in young believers in order to stem the growing trend of only a small portion of teen evangelicals holding on to their faith as adults. The increased media attention is putting the problem of generational faith transference in the spotlight and raising interest in effective responses.

College Is Not the Problem: Contrary to popular opinion, college is not the problem. In fact, of emerging adults, those who do not attend college drop out of religion at a slightly higher rate than those who do attend college. One recent study, for instance, using some of the best longitudinal data available, has shown that it is not those who attend college but in fact those who do not attend college who are the most likely to experience declines in religious service attendance, self-reported importance of religion, and religious affiliation.[5] Another study showed that among recently surveyed college students, 2.7 times more reported that their religious beliefs had strengthened during their college experience than said their beliefs weakened.[6] In every case, emerging adults currently in college are slightly more religious than those who are not in college.

Student Ministries Are Not the Problem: Some have pointed the finger of blame at age-graded student ministry in churches. But James Shields begs to differ, pointing to a 2008 survey of several hundred young adults who had been active in a megachurch student ministry as teens and remained somewhat active.[7] Most claimed to have continued attending church on a fairly regular basis, although less than while living at home.

Age of Conversion: About 65 percent of those who become believers in Jesus Christ do so as minors. Children ages five to thirteen have a 32 percent probability of coming to Christ. Those in and beyond their teens have a 4 to 5 percent probability.[8] This observation was reinforced by a separate study conducted by a University of Notre Dame team. Nearly one-third of emerging adults surveyed by the Center for the Study of Religion and Society made *no* religious commitment by age twenty-three.[9] The vast majority of those who had made a commitment to live their lives for God appeared to have made their first commitment well before the age of fourteen. These findings complement and reinforce one of the larger stories of this book: that the religious commitments and orientations of most people appear to be set early in life and very likely follow a consistent trajectory from that early formation through the adolescent and into the emerging adult years. Most people are set early in life to follow one religious trajectory or another—mostly, as we showed earlier, formed by the religious lives of their parents.

Faith Commitment Timing:

- No Faith Commitment: 31 percent
- Committed before Age Fourteen: 59 percent
- New Teen Commitments: 5 percent
- Emerging Adult Commitments: 5 percent

Faith Retention Rates: The same study revealed that 17 percent of emerging adults became more religiously active than they were during high school, while 55 percent backed away from active faith. Among those who continued to associate with a childhood tradition, some groups show higher retention rates than others:

- Latter-Day Saints: 72 percent retained
- Nonreligious: 68 percent
- Roman Catholic: 66 percent
- Conservative Protestant: 64 percent
- Jewish: 61 percent
- Other Religions: 60 percent
- Black Protestant: 55 percent
- Mainline Protestant: 50 percent[10]

Marriage, Parenthood, and Faith: The 2009 book *Souls in Transition* summarizes a longitudinal study of "emerging adults" ages eighteen to twenty-three conducted by the Center for the Study of Religion and Society at the University of Notre Dame. The study found that marriage, children, and religion tend to go together, at least in the United States.[11] So the more marriage and children are delayed, the more religious involvement is postponed and perhaps never reengaged (if ever engaged in the first place). One of the strongest factors that brings young adult Americans back to religion after a probable hiatus during emerging adulthood is forming new families and especially having children. In the causally reverse direction, being more religious also makes people more likely to marry at all, to marry earlier, to have children at all, and to bear them at a younger age—thus, the strong family-religion connection in the United States is mutually reinforcing, even synergistic. All else being equal, then, we can say that the younger Americans are when they marry and bear children, the more religious they are likely to be. So the postponement of "settling down" that is associated with emerging adulthood unintentionally produces, as a causal mechanism, the tendency for Americans to reduce religious involvements during this phase of life.

Leaving and Returning: The Southern Baptist Convention (SBC) is America's largest Protestant denomination. In recent years, conflicting statistics have surfaced about generational faith transference—the most dramatic claiming that 94 percent of kids abandon the church after graduating from high school. As many expected, that claim proved an exaggeration. Authors Thom and Sam Rainer conducted research among Southern Baptist young adults, which revealed that about 70 percent drop out between the ages of eighteen and twenty-two. The vast majority stop attending church because of a change such as moving away from home, attending college, or starting a career. The good news is that about two-thirds of the 70 percent who drop out come back, although their attendance is much less regular. What brought them back to church? The most common reasons given, not surprisingly, were "getting married" and "having children." The 30 percent who did not drop out of church were much more likely to grow up in a home with parents who remained married to each other, gave their children direct spiritual guidance, discussed spiritual matters, and/ or prayed with them. Most of those who remained active attended church with their parents. Most of those who dropped out went to a different church than their parents did. In short, they attended church when young with their parents and came back with a spouse and children of their own.[12] Clearly, marriage and parenthood serve as the glue connecting us to active faith.

Historic Trends: In her book *How the West Really Lost God*, Hoover Institute's Mary Eberstadt demonstrated how a society that moves away from the priority of family drives itself further from God. "Something about the family inclines people toward religiosity."[13] She showed that in Western Europe, unprecedented family shrinkage (decline in marriage and parenthood) appeared sometimes before and sometimes in tandem with the unprecedented decline in belief. In light of historical precedence, Eberstadt suggested that motherhood and fatherhood strengthen spiritual commitment because they are "the human symphony through which God has historically been heard by many people"[14] and that family and children are the means "through which people derive their deepest opinions and impressions of life."[15]

Decline in Parenthood: A 2006 essay called "Life without Children" examines how a delay in parenting, decline in births, and devaluing of parenthood is making America less child-centered. It states,

> We are in the midst of a profound change in American life. Demographically, socially and culturally, the nation is shifting from a society of child-rearing families to a society of child-free adults. The percentage of households with children has declined from half of all households in 1960 to less than one-third today—the lowest percentage in the nation's history. Indeed, if the twentieth century aspired to become the "century of the child,"

the twenty-first may well become the century of the
child-free.…

It is hard enough to rear children in a society
that is organized to support that essential social task.
Consider how much more difficult it becomes when
a society is indifferent at best, and hostile at worst,
to those who are caring for the next generation.[16]

What Fueled the "Seeker" Movement?: To some degree, the
church-growth movement of the past few decades helped slow the
decline of Christian faith in America. Once again, however, that
movement's engine was family formation. "Churches are full of
people who left church as single, young adults and returned to the
pews when they had families of their own," writes religion reporter
Paul Asay.[17] Why? University of Chicago professor Dr. Leon Kass
said it like this: "It is fatherhood and motherhood that teach most
of us what it took to bring us into our own adulthood. And it is the
desire to give not only life but a *good way of life* to our children that
opens us toward a serious concern for the true, the good, and even
the holy. Parental love of children leads once wayward sheep back
into the fold of church."[18]

Toward a "Sticky" Faith

Even the most conservative reports suggest that Christianity has
become less "sticky" than it was in past generations. And the reason,
in our view, is because we have been neglecting the primary engines
of lifelong faith: marriage and parenthood.

This is why we have become part of the dialogue with a network of innovative pastors who agree that the home must become a key strategic priority for the local church. The Strong Families Innovation Alliance includes leaders from some of the nation's most respected churches and about a dozen other congregations of various sizes and traditions. We invited the full range of pastoral perspectives, including senior and executive pastors, teaching and small-group pastors, spiritual formation and discipleship pastors, and student and children's pastors. This group of leaders cooperated together to clarify goals, identify challenges, and develop workable strategies to help the church inspire family intentionality.

The first step in helping churches become intentional about spiritual formation at home is defining the problem and clarifying the goals. Prior to the first gathering, Strong Families Innovation Alliance participants approved the following summary as a common target for innovation.

PROBLEM STATEMENT

Evangelical families are failing to win and keep their own children in the Christian faith.

VISION

To create a movement among evangelical churches that seeks to turn the tide by acknowledging the home as central to God's redemptive strategy.

INNOVATION TARGETS

- **Strengthening Marriages:** Children need to experience a loving relationship between Mom and Dad as a picture of the gospel. This foundation dramatically increases the likelihood that kids will want to embrace their parents' beliefs.
- **Winning Our Children to Christ:** The overwhelming majority of those who ever become Christians do so as children, most before age thirteen. Most parents recognize that it is their job to pass the Christian faith to their kids in the context of the home, yet they feel ill equipped to do so.
- **Launching Our Youth:** An alarmingly high percentage of teens raised in Christian families abandon their parents' faith during the teen and young adult years. And while this trend has created tension between parents and youth ministers, partnership between church and home is vital to launching our youth as committed believers.

UNDERSTANDING THE PRESENT REALITY

After crafting language to describe the problem and innovation targets, we assessed the current reality in our churches. The majority of participants indicated they had a "strong desire" to make a difference in the lives of members and attendees by using "periodic programs and some participation." None, however, believed they had a "compelling vision with effective programs and high participation." They summarized the present reality with regard to church-driven family ministry in five brief statements....

1. FAMILY MINISTRY = CHILDREN'S MINISTRY

Unfortunately, when church leaders hear "family ministry," they typically limit their thinking to "children's ministry." As a result, very few develop high-level strategies to drive marriage or parenting intentionality.

2. MARRIAGE MINISTRY = ANNUAL EVENT

Similarly, when church leaders hear "marriage ministry," they tend to think of an annual retreat or event rather than an ongoing strategy for building God-honoring marriages.

3. BEST CASE = SECONDARY PRIORITY

Most church leaders acknowledge that family-oriented ministry is a second- or third-tier priority in their church.

4. WORSE CASE = OFF THE RADAR SCREEN

Many churches do not even have a value statement about the home, so programs driving family intentionality are completely off the strategic radar screen.

5. NEED = INTEGRATED STRATEGIES

While many churches have created isolated programs for families—often in the form of life-stage classes that separate rather than integrate family faith experiences—what we need are integrated strategies that will create an ongoing culture of intentional families.

EFFECTIVE STRATEGIES

So how do we move toward integrated strategies? The Innovation Alliance identified ten components that are essential to building a customized strategy for church-driven, family-centered redemption. Consider these the ten "Lego piece" shapes essential to any model.

1. **Empower a Visionary Champion:** If everyone owns it, no one does. Make it clear which senior leader is responsible for keeping objectives for spiritual formation at home on the team's radar screen.

2. **Establish New Success Measures:** What gets measured gets done. Introduce simple measures that will keep you focused on family-centered strategies and drive continual improvement.

3. **Build upon Existing Church Vision:** Do not compete with or criticize the existing vision. Build upon it to drive family-centered strategies. Don't call the church to change everything—but to make everything more effective.

4. **Build It into the Existing Church Calendar:** Include experiences on the church calendar that will move people toward

greater intentionality rather than try to squeeze things in as exceptions or special events. The more "autopilot" your family emphasis game plan, the easier it will be for everyone.

5. **Use "Home" Lens for All versus Creating New Silo:** As a priority, every area of the church must own and apply "faith at home" lenses to every department and program rather than creating another silo competing for attention and resources.

6. **Define Success and Call Families to Commitment:** Give families a vision of what success at home means, and repeatedly call them to commitment and intentionality.

7. **Foster a Culture of Family Intentionality:** Find ways to communicate the priority and celebrate the practice of families becoming intentional.

8. **Customization: One Size Won't Fit All:** Every family is unique because of life-season, ages and number of children, marital health, special circumstances, etc. Provide tools that make it easy for families to customize.

9. **Invest in Tools for Families:** Just like we invest in curriculum for Sunday school, we need to invest in tools that will make it easier for families to do the right thing.

10. **Two-Degree Strategies:** A good plan today is better than a perfect plan tomorrow. It is better to start small and build momentum than try to change everything all at once or achieve complete buy-in from all sectors.

Using these ten "Lego piece" shapes, Alliance churches went on to create a variety of models that fit their unique needs. They learned that there is no cookie-cutter approach for churches that want to nurture lifelong faith in their members. But it is helpful to learn from the model pioneered at Lake Pointe Church that we have adapted to our own culture and context here at Calvary Chapel Chino Hills.

One of the challenges for any strategic initiative is defining success. It can be difficult and burdensome for the typical church to create elaborate systems to measure qualitative impact—especially when there are so many variables in each family. That's why we decided to keep the definition of success simple: to create a culture of intentional families. How? By consistently doing three things ...

STRATEGY #1: CAST A VISION

One of our responsibilities as leaders is to declare a new paradigm to the families attending our churches. They need us to cast a vision of what it means to be an intentional family. Why do Christian families outsource the spiritual formation of children to the "professionals" at church? Because church leaders have failed to clarify that lifelong faith is best nurtured in the home. That's why we should pour our best creativity into reminding our people that God designed the family as the primary context of faith formation. I created a one-page summary called "The Point of Home," which gives a quick overview of the "what" and "why" of our strategy.

THE POINT OF HOME—IN BRIEF

Most of us are called to worship God through the intimacy of marriage and the blessing of children. So we must understand Christian teaching on the purpose and priority of the home, which is summarized as follows …

- **SHOW CHRIST:** Every marriage is intended to be a masterpiece reflecting *the* marriage between God and His people (Gen. 1:27; Gen. 15; Jer. 3; Eph. 5:22–33; Rev. 21:9).

"For this reason a man will leave his father and mother and be united to his wife, and the two will become one flesh." This is a profound mystery—but I am talking about Christ and the church. However, each of you also must love his wife as he loves himself, and the wife must respect her husband. (Eph. 5:31–33 NIV)

- **RAISE BELIEVERS:** Those blessed with the gift of children are called to disciple the next generation as life's greatest priority (Exod. 20; Deut. 6; Ps. 78:1–8; Eph. 6:1–4).

He commanded our ancestors to teach their children, so the next generation would know them, even the children yet to be born, and they in turn would tell their children. Then they would put their trust in God. (Ps. 78:5–7 NIV)

- **BE JESUS:** A strong Christian family is where *the Word* becomes *Flesh and Blood* as we conform our lives to the image and example of Christ (John 1:14; Phil. 2; 1 Tim. 3; 1 John 3:16).

This is how we know what love is: Jesus Christ laid
down his life for us. And we ought to lay down our lives
for our brothers and sisters. (1 John 3:16 NIV)

In light of these priorities we will consistently call our people
to …

- **HONOR MARRIAGE:** Pursue a God-honoring marriage
  by giving themselves to a husband or wife through mutual
  submission and faithful devotion.
- **PASS THE FAITH:** Intentionally disciple their own
  children and grandchildren by capturing and creating experiences that deepen the roots of faith.
- **WALK THE TALK:** Live their faith at home in ways that
  will attract the next generation and the next-door neighbor
  to Christ.

STRATEGY #2: MAKE IT EASY

We try to make it as easy as possible for families to become intentional at home by providing practical tools for intentionality. Calvary
Chapel Chino Hills created a physical and online version of the
@HOME Center, where people can stop by to pick up free audio and
print resources designed to inspire and equip them toward building
a God-honoring home one step at a time. Every household has a
different dynamic. That's why families need customized tools. We
provide them with advice in nearly thirty family-season categories,
including singles wondering whether they should marry, widows who

have lost a spouse of fifty years, and everything in between. We try to give them a biblical perspective on whatever season of family life they find themselves in and offer practical suggestions for becoming more intentional in the coming days. We also provide free date-night ideas, family-time activities, parent-teen movie night questions to foster faith discussions using popular films, holiday intentionality suggestions, and many other resources that make it easy to do the right thing at home.

STRATEGY #3: MAKE IT MORE LIKELY

Calvary Chapel Chino Hills seeks to increase the probability that families in our church will become intentional by coordinating trimester campaigns in which we invite all families to create a 120-day intentionality plan. Just like every church plans a special "campaign" for Christmas, Easter, and other special events on the calendar, we have built into the church calendar at least three weekends in which the pastor and staff inspire families to create a simple plan. Sometimes the campaign is attached to a sermon series (i.e., Building Strong Families) or season of the year (i.e., Easter@Home, Summer@Home). Other times, all of the ministries cooperate to inspire attendees to start one simple "holy habit" such as Prayer@Home, The Blessing@Home, or Families Serving Together.

This approach is rooted in a conversation I had with former secretary of the interior Don Hodel about "The Law of Seven Mentionings." While serving on Ronald Reagan's cabinet, Don learned something about leaders. The first time Don raised an idea with Reagan he found that the president might dismiss or dislike the suggestion. By the seventh mentioning, however, the president thought it was his own idea!

Advertising agencies understand this principle also. They know that effective marketing includes something they call "frequency and reach." It typically takes hearing a message four, five, or six times before people take action—be it buying a product or calling a toll-free number. Much the same occurs when casting a new vision with people in the church. Many will readily jump on board with the idea of faith formation at home. Others will dismiss or dislike the suggestion. That's why we keep coming back to the same idea in various ways. Each time, more people take action at home. We have found that trimester campaigns allow us to leverage the Law of Seven Mentionings by creating an ongoing culture of family intentionality.

Churches like Calvary Chapel Chino Hills try to leverage existing time slots for the greatest possible impact with the least possible disruption to existing processes and programs. They customized a model any church can replicate within about 120 days—typically with strong buy-in by a cross section of ministry owners. Visit DriveFaithHome.com to view video clips and request additional information about that.

INTENTIONAL LEADERSHIP

Once upon a time, some church leader came up with a breakthrough concept called "liturgy" to give an eclectic network of believers a common language and pattern for worship.

Centuries later, Protestant reformers invented a brand-new process called "catechism" in response to widespread ignorance of basic Christian beliefs. Even more radical, they translated the Scriptures into the common tongue and encouraged people to read the Bible for themselves.

In an era when orphans needed biblical instruction because they had no parents to provide it at home, churches launched a groundbreaking solution called "Sunday school."

We don't tend to view ideas older than five years as innovative. But when viewed in light of their time, we see just how radically new each idea was. Someone saw a problem that needed a solution and took the initiative to lead. As a result, the list of ministry innovations driven by necessity goes on and on—from church hymnals filled with doctrine to church websites giving directions; from icons picturing saints to iPods playing sermons; from choirs wearing robes to bands beating drums; and from large meeting cathedrals to small-group DVDs. In each case, a change was driven by necessity.

The time has come for those called to lead God's church in our generation to find innovative solutions to what may be the most significant challenge of our time. We are bringing our kids to great churches, yet they are rejecting Christianity at an alarming rate. As we've said before, the problem is not what's happening during the one or two hours we have them at church. The problem is what desperately needs to happen in our homes.

Our prayer is that thousands of innovative leaders will become radically creative about forming a culture of intentional families. We need to fan the flame of innovation and apply our best thinking to the problem of declining generational faith transfer. That process will happen only when church leaders recognize the family as central to God's redemptive strategy. Remember, nurturing lifelong faith starts at home.

Join the movement at
DriveFaithHome.com

NOTES

CHAPTER FOUR: YOUR HERITAGE

1. Gary Oliver and H. Norman Wright, *When Anger Hits Home* (Chicago: Moody Press, 1992), 69, 29.

CHAPTER FIVE: YOUR SPIRITUAL LEGACY

1. Noah Webster, *An American Dictionary of the English Language (1828)*, s.v. *"legacy."*

CHAPTER SEVEN: YOUR SOCIAL LEGACY

1. Dale Carnegie, *How to Win Friends and Influence People* (New York: Simon & Schuster, 1998), xvi.

2. *Minnesota Crime Commission Report*, quoted in Charles R. Swindoll, *Growing Wise in Family Life* (Portland, OR: Multnomah, 1988), 102.

APPENDIX

1. Barry A. Kosmin, Egon Mayer, and Ariela Keysar, "American Religious Identification Survey," The Graduate Center of the City University of New York, December 19, 2001, http://www.gc.cuny.edu/CUNY_GC/media/CUNY-Graduate-Center/PDF/ARIS/ARIS-PDF-version.pdf.

2. Jon Meacham, "The End of Christian America," *Newsweek*, April 3, 2009, http://www.thedailybeast.com/newsweek/2009/04/03/the-end-of-christian-america.html.

3. David Kinnaman and Gabe Lyons, *unChristian* (Grand Rapids, MI: Baker Books, 2007), 74.

4. Laurie Goodstein, "Evangelicals Fear the Loss of Their Teenagers," *New York Times*, October 6, 2006, http://www.nytimes.com/2006/10/06/us/06evangelical.html?hp&ex=1160107200&en=4bc2ab121e996b11&ei=5094&partner=homepage&_r=0.

5. Kinnaman and Lyons, *unChristian*.

6. Christian Smith, *Souls in Transition* (Oxford University Press, 2009), 248–49.

7. James Shields, *An Assessment of Dropout Raters of Former Youth Ministry Participants in Conservative Southern Baptist Megachurches* (The Southern Baptist Theological Seminary, 2008).

8. The Barna Group, "Evangelism Is Most Effective Among Kids," *The Barna Update*, October 11, 2004, https://www.barna.org/barna-update/article/5-barna-update/196-evangelism-is-most-effective-among-kids#.UdtD34WOOB0.

9. Smith, *Souls in Transition* (Oxford University Press, 2009).

10. Smith, *Souls in Transition*.

11. Smith, *Souls in Transition*, 79.

12. Thom Rainer and Sam Rainer, *Essential Church?* (Nashville: B&H, 2008).

13. Mary Eberstadt, *How the West Really Lost God* (West Conshohocken, PA: Templeton Press, 2013), 100.

14. Eberstadt, *How the West Really Lost God*, 216.

15. Mary Eberstadt, "How the West Really Lost God," *Policy Review* 143 (June–July 2007).

16. *The State of Our Unions 2006: The Social Health of Marriage in America*, The National Marriage Project, July 2006, www.stateofourunions.org/pdfs/SOOU2006.pdf.

17. "Life without Children," *The State of Our Unions 2006: The Social Health of Marriage in America*.

18. Leon Kass, "The End of Courtship," *The Public Interest*, Winter 1997, http://www.nationalaffairs.com/public_interest/detail/the-end-of-courtship.